Table of Contents

I0427889

(Continued)

Part One
Why Employers Must Verify Employment Authorization and Identity of New Employees

In 1986, Congress reformed U.S. immigration laws. These reforms, the result of a bipartisan effort, preserved the tradition of legal immigration while seeking to close the door to illegal entry. The employer sanctions provisions, found in section 274A of the Immigration and Nationality Act (INA), were added by the Immigration Reform and Control Act of 1986 (IRCA). These provisions further changed with the passage of the Immigration Act of 1990 and the Illegal Immigration Reform and Immigrant Responsibility Act (IIRIRA) of 1996.

Employment is often the magnet that attracts individuals to reside in the United States illegally. The purpose of the employer sanctions law is to remove this magnet by requiring employers to hire only individuals who may legally work here: U.S. citizens, noncitizen nationals, lawful permanent residents, and aliens authorized to work. To comply with the law, employers must verify the identity and employment authorization of each person they hire, complete and retain a Form I-9, *Employment Eligibility Verification,* for each employee, and refrain from discriminating against individuals on the basis of national origin or citizenship. (See Part Four for more information on unlawful discrimination.)

Form I-9 helps employers to verify individuals who are authorized to work in the United States. You, as an employer, must complete a Form I-9 for every new employee you hire after November 6, 1986.

This Handbook provides guidance on how to properly complete Form I-9 and answers frequently asked questions about the law as it relates to Form I-9.

The Homeland Security Act

The Homeland Security Act of 2002 created an executive department combining numerous federal agencies with a mission dedicated to homeland security. On March 1, 2003, the authorities of the former Immigration and Naturalization Service (INS) were transferred to three new agencies in the U.S. Department of Homeland Security (DHS): U.S. Citizenship and Immigration Services (USCIS), U.S. Customs and Border Protection (CBP), and U.S. Immigration and Customs Enforcement (ICE). The two DHS immigration components most involved with the matters discussed in this Handbook are USCIS and ICE. USCIS is responsible for most documentation of alien employment authorization, for Form I-9, and for the E-Verify employment eligibility verification program. ICE is responsible for enforcement of the penalty provisions of section 274A of the INA and for other immigration enforcement within the United States.

Under the Homeland Security Act, the U. S. Department of Justice (DOJ) retained certain important responsibilities related to Form I-9 as well. In particular, the Office of Special Counsel for Immigration-Related Unfair Employment Practices (OSC) in the Civil Rights Division is responsible for enforcement of the anti-discrimination provision in section 274B of the INA, while the Executive Office for Immigration Review (EOIR) is responsible for the administrative adjudication of cases under sections 274A, 274B, and 274C (civil document fraud) of the INA.

Page intentionally left blank

Part Two
Completing Form I-9

You must complete Form I-9 each time you hire any person to perform labor or services in the United States in return for wages or other remuneration. Remuneration is anything of value given in exchange for labor or services, including food and lodging. The requirement to complete Form I-9 applies to new employees hired after November 6, 1986. This requirement does not apply to employees hired on or before November 6, 1986, who are continuing in their employment and have a reasonable expectation of employment at all times.

Ensure that the employee completes Section 1 of Form I-9 at the time of hire. "Hire" means when employment in exchange for wages or other remuneration begins. The time of hire is noted on the form as the first day of employment. Employees may complete Section 1 of Form I-9 before the time of hire, but no earlier than acceptance of the job offer. Review the employee's document(s) and fully complete Section 2 of Form I-9 within three business days of the hire. For example, if the employee begins employment on Monday, you must complete Section 2 by Thursday.

If you hire a person for fewer than three business days, Sections 1 and 2 of Form I-9 must be fully completed at the time of hire – in other words, by the first day employment for pay begins.

You may not begin the Form I-9 process until you offer an individual a job and he or she accepts your offer.

You DO NOT complete a Form I-9 for persons who are:

1. Hired on or before November 6, 1986, (on or before November 27, 2009 if employment is in the Commonwealth of the Northern Mariana Islands (CNMI)) who are continuing in their employment and have a reasonable expectation of employment at all times; (This exception to the requirement does not apply to seasonal employees or employees who change employers within a multi-employer association. Other limitations may also apply.)

2. Employed for casual domestic work in a private home on a sporadic, irregular, or intermittent basis;

3. Independent contractors;

4. Providing labor to you who are employed by a contractor providing contract services (e.g., employee leasing or temporary agencies); or

5. Not physically working on U.S. soil.

NOTE: You cannot contract for the labor of an individual if you know that he or she is not authorized to work in the United States.

Completing Section 1

Have the employee complete Section 1 at the time of hire (i.e., by the first day that his or her employment for pay begins) by filling in the correct information and signing and dating the form. Ensure that the employee prints the information clearly.

If the employee cannot complete Section 1 without assistance or if he or she needs Form I-9 translated, someone may assist him or her. The preparer or translator must read the form to the employee, assist him or her in completing Section 1 and have the employee sign or mark the form in the appropriate place. The preparer or translator must then complete the Preparer and/or Translator Certification Block on Form I-9. If the employee requires multiple preparers and/or translators, subsequent preparers and/or translators must complete the Preparer/Translator Certification Block of a new Form I-9 (one per person) and attach that page to the employee's form.

You are responsible for reviewing and ensuring that your employee fully and properly completes Section 1.

NOTE: Providing a Social Security number on Form I-9 is voluntary for all employees unless you are an employer participating in the USCIS E-Verify program. Providing an e-mail address or telephone number is voluntary.

You may not ask an employee to provide you a specific document with his or her Social Security number on it. To do so may constitute unlawful discrimination. For more information on E-Verify, see Part Six. For more information on unlawful discrimination, see Part Four.

Section 1. Employee Information and Attestation *(Employees must complete and sign Section 1 of Form I-9 no later than the **first day of employment**, but not before accepting a job offer.)*

Last Name (Family Name)	First Name (Given Name)	Middle Initial	Other Names Used (if any)		
Doe	John	A	N/A		

Address (Street Number and Name)	Apt. Number	City or Town	State	Zip Code
123 Main Street	1	Washington	DC	20000

Date of Birth (mm/dd/yyyy)	U.S. Social Security Number	E-mail Address	Telephone Number
01/01/1960	0 0 0 - 0 0 - 0 0 0 0	johndoe@email.com	(202) 123-4567

I am aware that federal law provides for imprisonment and/or fines for false statements or use of false documents in connection with the completion of this form.

I attest, under penalty of perjury, that I am (check one of the following):

☐ A citizen of the United States

☐ A noncitizen national of the United States *(See instructions)*

☐ A lawful permanent resident (Alien Registration Number/USCIS Number): _____

☒ An alien authorized to work until (expiration date, if applicable, mm/dd/yyyy) 02/28/2015 _____ . Some aliens may write "N/A" in this field. *(See instructions)*

For aliens authorized to work, provide your Alien Registration Number/USCIS Number **OR** Form I-94 Admission Number:

1. Alien Registration Number/USCIS Number: 1 2 3 4 5 6 7 8 9 _____

OR

2. Form I-94 Admission Number: _____

If you obtained your admission number from CBP in connection with your arrival in the United States, include the following:

Foreign Passport Number: _____

Country of Issuance: _____

Some aliens may write "N/A" on the Foreign Passport Number and Country of Issuance fields. *(See instructions)*

> 3-D Barcode
> Do Not Write in This Space

Signature of Employee: *John A. Doe*	Date (mm/dd/yyyy): 06/30/2013

Preparer and/or Translator Certification *(To be completed and signed if Section 1 is prepared by a person other than the employee.)*

I attest, under penalty of perjury, that I have assisted in the completion of this form and that to the best of my knowledge the information is true and correct.

Signature of Preparer or Translator: *Jane Doe*	Date (mm/dd/yyyy): 06/30/2013

Last Name (Family Name)	First Name (Given Name)		
Doe	Jane		

Address (Street Number and Name)	City or Town	State	Zip Code
123 Main Street	Washington	DC	20000

Figure 1: Completing Section 1: Employee Information and Verification

(1) Enter your full legal name and other names that you have used in the past or present (e.g., maiden name) if any.

- If you have two last names (family names), include both in the Last Name field. If you hyphenate your last name, include the hyphen (-) between the names.

- If you have two first names (given names), include both in the First Name field. If you hyphenate your first name, include the hyphen (-) between the names.

- If you have only one name, enter that name in the Last Name field. You may enter either the word "Unknown" or "N/A" in the First Name field. If your employer is an E-Verify participant, entering "Unknown" is preferable. You may not leave this field blank.

- Enter your middle initial in the Middle Initial field, if applicable. Enter N/A if you have no middle initial.

- Enter your maiden name or any other legal name you may have used in the Other Names Used field. Enter N/A if you have not used other names.

(2) Enter your home Address, Apt. Number, City or Town, State and Zip Code. Enter N/A if you have no Apt. Number. You may not enter a P.O. Box in this field. If you have no street address, enter a description of the location of your residence, such as "9 miles south of I-81, to the left of the water tower."

(3) Enter your Date of Birth, Social Security Number, E-mail Address and Telephone Number. Entering the Social Security number is optional unless your employer confirms employment authorization using E-Verify. Entering your e-mail address or telephone number is voluntary. If you choose not to enter your e-mail address or telephone number, enter N/A in these fields.

(4) Read the warning and attest to your citizenship or immigration status by checking the appropriate box. If you attest to 'Alien authorized to work,' you may provide EITHER your Alien Registration number OR your Form I-94 Admission Number. If you choose to provide an Alien Registration Number, you do not have to enter your Foreign Passport and Country of Issuance information.

(5) Sign and date the form.

(6) If you use a preparer or translator to fill out the form, that person must certify that he or she assisted you by completing the Preparer and/or Translator Certification Block. If you require multiple preparers and/or translators, subsequent preparers and/or translators must complete the Preparer/Translator Certification of a second Form I-9 and attach that page to your form.

Completing Section 2

The employee must present to you an original document or documents that show his or her identity and employment authorization within three business days of the date employment begins. For example, if the employee begins employment on Monday, you must complete Section 2 by Thursday. Some documents show both identity and employment authorization (List A). Other documents show identity only (List B) or employment authorization only (List C). The employee must be allowed to choose which document(s) he or she wants to present from the Lists of Acceptable Documents. These lists appear in Part Eight and on the last page of Form I-9.

Physically examine each original document(s) the employee presents to determine if it reasonably appears to be genuine and to relate to the person presenting it. The person who examines the documents must be the same person who signs Section 2. The employee must be physically present with the examiner of the documents during the examination of the employee's documents. You must examine one document from List A, or one from List B **AND** one from List C. Enter the title, issuing authority, number, and expiration date (if any) of the document(s); fill in the date employment begins and correct information in the certification block; and sign and date Form I-9. You must accept any document(s) from the Lists of Acceptable Documents presented by the individual that reasonably appear on their face to be genuine and to relate to the person presenting them. You may not specify which document(s) an employee must present. However, you may only accept unexpired documents. If you choose to make copies of documents your employee presents, you must do so for all employees, regardless of national origin or citizenship status. Return the original documents to your employee when you are finished.

NOTE: If you participate in E-Verify, you may only accept List B documents that bear a photograph.

Section 2. Employer or Authorized Representative Review and Verification

(Employers or their authorized representative must complete and sign Section 2 within 3 business days of the employee's first day of employment. You must physically examine one document from List A OR examine a combination of one document from List B and one document from List C as listed on the "Lists of Acceptable Documents" on the next page of this form. For each document you review, record the following information: document title, issuing authority, document number, and expiration date, if any.)

(1) Employee Last Name, First Name and Middle Initial from Section 1: Doe, John A

List A	OR	List B	AND	List C
Identity and Employment Authorization		Identity		Employment Authorization

(2)

List A	List B	List C
Document Title: EAD	Document Title:	Document Title:
Issuing Authority: DHS/USCIS	Issuing Authority:	Issuing Authority:
Document Number: XXX1234567891	Document Number:	Document Number:
Expiration Date (if any)(mm/dd/yyyy): 02/28/2015	Expiration Date (if any)(mm/dd/yyyy):	Expiration Date (if any)(mm/dd/yyyy):
Document Title:		
Issuing Authority:		
Document Number:		
Expiration Date (if any)(mm/dd/yyyy):		
Document Title:		
Issuing Authority:		
Document Number:		
Expiration Date (if any)(mm/dd/yyyy):		3-D Barcode Do Not Write in This Space

Certification

I attest, under penalty of perjury, that (1) I have examined the document(s) presented by the above-named employee, (2) the above-listed document(s) appear to be genuine and to relate to the employee named, and (3) to the best of my knowledge the employee is authorized to work in the United States.

(3) The employee's first day of employment *(mm/dd/yyyy):* 06/30/2013 **(See instructions for exemptions.)**

(4)

Signature of Employer or Authorized Representative *alice Smith*	Date *(mm/dd/yyyy)* 07/02/2013	Title of Employer or Authorized Representative HR Manager		
Last Name *(Family Name)* Smith	First Name *(Given Name)* Alice	Employer's Business or Organization Name Widgets, Inc.		

(5)

Employer's Business or Organization Address *(Street Number and Name)* 567 Maple Street	City or Town Washington	State DC	Zip Code 20000

Figure 2: Section 2: Employer or Authorized Representative Review and Verification

(1) Enter the employee's name from Section 1 at the top of Section 2.

(2) Enter the document title(s), issuing authority, document number, and the expiration date from original documents supplied by employee. You may use common abbreviations to document the document title or issuing authority, e.g. DL for driver's license and SSA for Social Security Administration.

NOTE: If the employee is a student or exchange visitor who presented a foreign passport with a Form I-94, the employer should also enter the student's Form I-20 or DS-2019 number (Student and Exchange Visitor Number – SEVIS Number); and the program end date from Form I-20 or DS-2019.

(3) Enter the first day of employment for wages or other remuneration (i.e., date of hire) in the space for "The employee's first day of employment (mm/dd/yyyy)." Recruiters and recruiters for a fee do not enter the employee's first day of employment.

④ Employer or authorized representative attests to physically examining the documents provided by signing and dating the signature and date fields.

⑤ Enter the business name and address.

In certain circumstances, employers, recruiters, and referrers for a fee must accept a receipt in lieu of a List A, List B, or a List C document if one is presented by an employee.

Acceptable receipts an employee can present are listed in Table 1 below.

When the employee provides an acceptable receipt, enter the document title in Section 2 of Form I-9, enter the word "receipt" and its document number in the "Document #" space, and enter the last day that the receipt is valid in the "Expiration Date" field. When the employee presents the actual document, cross out the word "receipt" and any accompanying document number and expiration date, insert the number from the actual document presented, and initial and date the change.

A receipt indicating that an individual has applied for an initial Employment Authorization Document (Form I-766) or for an extension of an expiring Employment Authorization Document (Form I-766) is NOT acceptable proof of employment authorization on Form I-9. Receipts are never acceptable if employment lasts fewer than three business days.

Table 1: Receipts

Receipt	Who may present this receipt?	Is this receipt proof of employment authorization and/or identity?	How long is this receipt valid?	What must the employee present at the end of the receipt validity period?
A receipt for a replacement of a lost, stolen, or damaged document	All employees	A receipt fulfills the verification requirements of the document for which the receipt was issued (can be List A, List B, or List C)	90 days from date of hire or, for reverification, the date employment authorization expires	The actual document for which the receipt was issued
The arrival portion of the Form I-94 or I-94A containing a Temporary I-551 stamp and photograph	Lawful Permanent Residents	Employment authorization and identity (List A)	Until the expiration date of the Temporary I-551 stamp or, if no expiration date, one year from date of issue	The actual Form I-551 (Permanent Resident Card, or "green card")
The departure portion of Form I-94 or I-94A with an unexpired refugee admission stamp	Refugees	Employment authorization and identity (List A)	90 days from date of hire or, for reverification, the date employment authorization expires	An unexpired EAD (Form I-766) or a combination of a valid List B document and an unrestricted Social Security card

Minors (Individuals under Age 18)

If a person under the age of 18 cannot present an identity document from List B, he or she may establish identity by completing Form I-9 as shown below.

Section 1. Employee Information and Attestation *(Employees must complete and sign Section 1 of Form I-9 no later than the **first day of employment**, but not before accepting a job offer.)*

Last Name *(Family Name)*	First Name *(Given Name)*	Middle Initial	Other Names Used *(if any)*
Doe	Susan	B	N/A

Address *(Street Number and Name)*	Apt. Number	City or Town	State	Zip Code
123 Minor Street	B	Washington	DC	20000

Date of Birth *(mm/dd/yyyy)*	U.S. Social Security Number	E-mail Address	Telephone Number
05/15/1999	0 0 0 - 0 0 - 0 0 0 0	susandoe@email.com	(202) 765-4321

I am aware that federal law provides for imprisonment and/or fines for false statements or use of false documents in connection with the completion of this form.

I attest, under penalty of perjury, that I am (check one of the following):

[X] A citizen of the United States

[ ] A noncitizen national of the United States *(See instructions)*

[ ] A lawful permanent resident (Alien Registration Number/USCIS Number): _____

[ ] An alien authorized to work until (expiration date, if applicable, mm/dd/yyyy) _____ . Some aliens may write "N/A" in this field. *(See instructions)*

For aliens authorized to work, provide your Alien Registration Number/USCIS Number **OR** Form I-94 Admission Number:

1. Alien Registration Number/USCIS Number: _____

OR

2. Form I-94 Admission Number: _____

If you obtained your admission number from CBP in connection with your arrival in the United States, include the following:

Foreign Passport Number: _____

Country of Issuance: _____

Some aliens may write "N/A" on the Foreign Passport Number and Country of Issuance fields. *(See instructions)*

3-D Barcode
Do Not Write in This Space

(1) | Signature of Employee: *Individual Under Age 18* | Date *(mm/dd/yyyy)*: 06/30/2013

Preparer and/or Translator Certification *(To be completed and signed if Section 1 is prepared by a person other than the employee.)*

I attest, under penalty of perjury, that I have assisted in the completion of this form and that to the best of my knowledge the information is true and correct.

(2) | Signature of Preparer or Translator: *Bill Doe* | Date *(mm/dd/yyyy)*: 06/30/2013

Last Name *(Family Name)*	First Name *(Given Name)*
Doe	Bill

Address *(Street Number and Name)*	City or Town	State	Zip Code
123 Minor Street	Washington	DC	20000

Figure 3: Completing Section 1 of Form I-9 for Minors without List B Documents

(1) Parent or legal guardian of a minor employee completes Section 1 and enter, "Individual under age 18" in signature block.

(2) Parent or legal guardian completes the Preparer and/or Translator Certification Block.

Section 2. Employer or Authorized Representative Review and Verification

(Employers or their authorized representative must complete and sign Section 2 within 3 business days of the employee's first day of employment. You must physically examine one document from List A OR examine a combination of one document from List B and one document from List C as listed on the "Lists of Acceptable Documents" on the next page of this form. For each document you review, record the following information: document title, issuing authority, document number, and expiration date, if any.)

(1) Employee Last Name, First Name and Middle Initial from Section 1: Doe, Susan B

List A	OR	List B	AND	List C
Identity and Employment Authorization		Identity		Employment Authorization

(2)

List A	List B	List C
Document Title:	Document Title: Individual under age 18	Document Title: Social Security Card
Issuing Authority:	Issuing Authority:	Issuing Authority: SSA
Document Number:	Document Number:	Document Number: 000000000
Expiration Date (if any)(mm/dd/yyyy):	Expiration Date (if any)(mm/dd/yyyy):	Expiration Date (if any)(mm/dd/yyyy): N/A
Document Title:		
Issuing Authority:		
Document Number:		
Expiration Date (if any)(mm/dd/yyyy):		
Document Title:		3-D Barcode
Issuing Authority:		Do Not Write in This Space
Document Number:		
Expiration Date (if any)(mm/dd/yyyy):		

Certification

I attest, under penalty of perjury, that (1) I have examined the document(s) presented by the above-named employee, (2) the above-listed document(s) appear to be genuine and to relate to the employee named, and (3) to the best of my knowledge the employee is authorized to work in the United States.

(3) The employee's first day of employment *(mm/dd/yyyy)*: 06/30/2013 **(See instructions for exemptions.)**

(4)

Signature of Employer or Authorized Representative *Mary Smith*	Date *(mm/dd/yyyy)* 07/01/2013	Title of Employer or Authorized Representative HR Manager
Last Name *(Family Name)* Smith	First Name *(Given Name)* Mary	Employer's Business or Organization Name Warm Coats, Inc.

(5)

Employer's Business or Organization Address *(Street Number and Name)* 456 S. Main Street	City or Town Washington	State DC	Zip Code 20000

Figure 4: Completing Section 2 of Form I-9 for Minors without List B Documents

(1) Enter the employee's name from Section 1 at the top of Section 2.

(2) Enter "Individual under age 18" under List B and enters the List C document the minor presents.

(3) Enter the date employment began.

(4) Employer or authorized representative attests to physically examining the documents provided by signing and dating the signature and date fields.

(5) Enter the business name and address.

Employees with Disabilities (Special Placement)

A person who has a physical or mental impairment which substantially limits one or more of such person's major life activities, and who is placed in a job by a nonprofit organization, association, or as part of a rehabilitation program, may establish identity under List B by using similar procedures to those used by persons under 18 years of age if he or she cannot produce a List B identity document and otherwise qualifies to use these procedures. Complete Form I-9 as shown below.

Section 1. Employee Information and Attestation (*Employees must complete and sign Section 1 of Form I-9 no later than the first day of employment, but not before accepting a job offer.*)

Last Name (*Family Name*)	First Name (*Given Name*)	Middle Initial	Other Names Used (*if any*)
Doe	Harold	T	N/A

Address (*Street Number and Name*)	Apt. Number	City or Town	State	Zip Code
123 Side Street	4	Washington	DC	20000

Date of Birth (*mm/dd/yyyy*)	U.S. Social Security Number	E-mail Address	Telephone Number
09/06/1977	0 0 0 - 0 0 - 0 0 0 0	harolddoe@email.com	(202) 765-4321

I am aware that federal law provides for imprisonment and/or fines for false statements or use of false documents in connection with the completion of this form.

I attest, under penalty of perjury, that I am (check one of the following):

[X] A citizen of the United States

[ ] A noncitizen national of the United States (*See instructions*)

[ ] A lawful permanent resident (Alien Registration Number/USCIS Number): _____

[ ] An alien authorized to work until (expiration date, if applicable, mm/dd/yyyy) _____ . Some aliens may write "N/A" in this field. (*See instructions*)

For aliens authorized to work, provide your Alien Registration Number/USCIS Number **OR** Form I-94 Admission Number:

1. Alien Registration Number/USCIS Number: _____

OR

2. Form I-94 Admission Number: _____

If you obtained your admission number from CBP in connection with your arrival in the United States, include the following:

Foreign Passport Number: _____

Country of Issuance: _____

Some aliens may write "N/A" on the Foreign Passport Number and Country of Issuance fields. (*See instructions*)

> 3-D Barcode
> Do Not Write in This Space

Signature of Employee: *Special Placement*	Date (*mm/dd/yyyy*): 06/30/2013

Preparer and/or Translator Certification (*To be completed and signed if Section 1 is prepared by a person other than the employee.*)

I attest, under penalty of perjury, that I have assisted in the completion of this form and that to the best of my knowledge the information is true and correct.

Signature of Preparer or Translator: *Bill Doe*	Date (*mm/dd/yyyy*): 06/30/2013

Last Name (*Family Name*)	First Name (*Given Name*)
Doe	Bill

Address (*Street Number and Name*)	City or Town	State	Zip Code
123 Cross Street	Washington	DC	20000

Figure 5: Completing Section 1 of Form I-9 for Employees with Disabilities (Special Placement)

(1) Representative of a nonprofit organization, parent, or legal guardian of an individual with a disability completes Section 1 and enters, "Special Placement" in the signature of employee field and dates the form.

(2) Representative, parent or legal guardian completes the Preparer and/or Translator Certification Block.

Section 2. Employer or Authorized Representative Review and Verification

(Employers or their authorized representative must complete and sign Section 2 within 3 business days of the employee's first day of employment. You must physically examine one document from List A OR examine a combination of one document from List B and one document from List C as listed on the "Lists of Acceptable Documents" on the next page of this form. For each document you review, record the following information: document title, issuing authority, document number, and expiration date, if any.)

① Employee Last Name, First Name and Middle Initial from Section 1: Doe, Harry T

List A Identity and Employment Authorization	OR	List B Identity	AND	List C Employment Authorization

②

List A	List B	List C
Document Title:	Document Title: Special Placement	Document Title: Social Security Card
Issuing Authority:	Issuing Authority:	Issuing Authority: SSA
Document Number:	Document Number:	Document Number: 000-00-0000
Expiration Date *(if any)(mm/dd/yyyy)*:	Expiration Date *(if any)(mm/dd/yyyy)*:	Expiration Date *(if any)(mm/dd/yyyy)*: N/A
Document Title:		
Issuing Authority:		
Document Number:		3-D Barcode Do Not Write in This Space
Expiration Date *(if any)(mm/dd/yyyy)*:		
Document Title:		
Issuing Authority:		
Document Number:		
Expiration Date *(if any)(mm/dd/yyyy)*:		

Certification

I attest, under penalty of perjury, that (1) I have examined the document(s) presented by the above-named employee, (2) the above-listed document(s) appear to be genuine and to relate to the employee named, and (3) to the best of my knowledge the employee is authorized to work in the United States.

③ The employee's first day of employment *(mm/dd/yyyy)*: 06/30/2013 _____ (See *instructions* for exemptions.)

④

Signature of Employer or Authorized Representative *Mary Smith*	Date *(mm/dd/yyyy)* 07/02/2013	Title of Employer or Authorized Representative HR Manager
Last Name *(Family Name)* Smith	First Name *(Given Name)* Mary	Employer's Business or Organization Name Warm Coats, Inc.

⑤

Employer's Business or Organization Address *(Street Number and Name)* 456 S. Main Street	City or Town Washington	State DC	Zip Code 20000

Figure 6: Completing Section 2 of Form I-9 for Employees with Disabilities (Special Placement)

① Enter the employee's name from Section 1 at the top of Section 2.

② Enter "Special Placement" under List B and enters the List C document that the employee with a disability presents.

③ Enter the date employment began.

④ Employer or authorized representative attests to physically examining the documents provided by signing and dating the signature and date fields.

⑤ Enter the business name and address.

Future Expiration Dates

Future expiration dates may appear on the employment authorization documents of individuals, including, among others, lawful permanent residents, asylees and refugees. USCIS includes expiration dates even on documents issued to individuals with permanent employment authorization. The existence of a future expiration date:

1. Does not preclude continuous employment authorization;

2. Does not mean that subsequent employment authorization will not be granted; and

3. Should not be considered in determining whether the individual is qualified for a particular position.

Considering a future employment authorization expiration date in determining whether an alien is qualified for a particular job may constitute employment discrimination. For more information on unlawful discrimination, see Part Four. However, as described below, you may need to reverify the employee's authorization to work when certain List A or List C documents expire. For example, the Employment Authorization Document (Form I-766) must be reverified on or before the expiration date.

Reverifying Employment Authorization for Current Employees

When an employee's employment authorization document expires, you must reverify his or her employment authorization no later than the date employment authorization expires. You may use Section 3 of Form I-9, or, if Section 3 has already been used for a previous reverification or update, use a new Form I-9. If you use a new Form I-9, enter the employee's name in the space provided at the top of Section 2, complete Section 3, and retain only the second page of the new Form I-9 with the original. The employee must present a document that shows current employment authorization, e.g., any document from List A or List C, including an unrestricted Social Security card. If the employee cannot provide you with proof of current employment authorization, you cannot continue to employ that person.

NOTE: U.S. citizens and noncitizen nationals never need reverification. Do not reverify the following documents: An expired U.S. passport or passport card, an Alien Registration Receipt Card/Permanent Resident Card (Form I-551), or a List B document that has expired.

Employees whose immigration status, employment authorization, or employment authorization documents expire should file the necessary application or petition sufficiently in advance to ensure that they maintain continuous employment authorization or valid employment authorization documents. If the employee is authorized to work for a specific employer, such as an H-1B or L-1 nonimmigrant, and has filed an application for an extension of stay, he or she may continue employment with the same employer for up to 240 days from the date the authorized period of stay expires. See *Completing Form I-9 for Nonimmigrant Categories* below.

NOTE: You must reverify an employee's employment authorization on Form I-9 no later than the date that the employee's employment authorization or employment authorization document expires, whichever is sooner.

Reverification and Evidence of Status for Certain Categories

Lawful Permanent Residents

Employees who attest to being a lawful permanent resident in Section 1 of Form I-9 may choose to present a valid Form I-551, Permanent Resident Card, for Section 2 (or Section 3, if applicable). A lawful permanent resident is not required to do so, however, and instead may choose to present a List B and List C document combination, e.g., state-issued driver's license and unrestricted Social Security card.

If an employee presents a Form I-551, you should know that Forms I-551 may contain no expiration date, a 10-year expiration date, or a two-year expiration date. Cards that expire in 10 years or not at all are issued to lawful permanent residents with no conditions on their status. Cards that expire in two years are issued to lawful permanent residents with conditions on their status. Conditional residents can lose their status if they fail to remove these conditions. Permanent Resident Cards with either an expiration date or no expiration date are List A documents that should not be reverified.

Lawful permanent residents and conditional residents may be issued temporary I-551 documents. These documents are acceptable for Form I-9 as follows:

1. If an employee presents an expired Permanent Resident Card along with a Form I-797, *Notice of Action*, that indicates that the card is valid for an additional year, this combination is acceptable List C evidence of employment authorization for one year as indicated on Form I-797. At the end of the one-year period, you must reverify.

2. If an employee presents a foreign passport with either a temporary I-551 stamp or I-551 printed notation on a machine-readable immigrant visa (MRIV), you must reverify when the stamp or MRIV expires, or one year after the issuance date if the stamp or MRIV does not contain an expiration date.

3. If an employee presents the arrival portion of Form I-94/Form I-94A containing an unexpired temporary I-551 stamp and a photograph of the individual, this combination of documents is an acceptable List A receipt for the Permanent Resident Card. The employee must present his or her Permanent Resident Card to the employer no later than when the stamp expires, or one year after the issuance date of the Form I-94 if the stamp does not contain an expiration date.

NOTE: If USCIS has approved the employee's application to adjust status to that of a lawful permanent resident, but the employee has not yet received his or her initial Form I-551, he or she can obtain temporary evidence of permanent resident status at a local USCIS field office. However, you may not accept Form I-797 that acknowledges receipt of an application for an initial Form I-551. Receipts showing an application for a new document are acceptable only if the original document has been lost, stolen, or damaged.

Refugees and Asylees

Refugees and asylees are authorized to work because of their immigration status. When completing Form I-9, the refugee or asylee should indicate "alien authorized to work" in Section 1 of Form I-9. Since refugees and asylees are authorized to work because of their immigration status, a refugee or asylee should enter "N/A" on the line calling for an expiration date.

Many refugees and asylees may choose to present an unexpired Employment Authorization Document (Form I-766) to employers to complete Form I-9. However, neither refugees nor asylees are required to present an Employment Authorization Document (Form I-766) to meet Form I-9 requirements. Both refugees and asylees may also present other documents that are acceptable for Form I-9, such as Form I-94/Form I-94A indicating refugee or asylee status. List B and List C combinations, such as a State-issued driver's license and an unrestricted Social Security card, may also be presented by both.

NOTE: The Social Security Administration issues refugees and asylees unrestricted Social Security cards. These are List C documents for Form I-9 purposes and are not subject to reverification. Application procedures for Social Security cards can be found on the Social Security Administration's site at www.ssa.gov.

Refugees

Upon admission to the United States, a refugee will receive Form I-94/Form I-94A with an unexpired refugee admission stamp. If an employee presents this document to complete Form I-9, the employer must accept it as a receipt establishing both employment authorization and identity for 90 days. In the meantime, USCIS will be processing an Employment Authorization Document (Form I-766) for the refugee.

At the end of the 90-day receipt period, the refugee must present either an Employment Authorization Document (Form I-766) or a document from List B, such as a State-issued driver's license, with a document from List C, such as an unrestricted Social Security card.

Asylees

After being granted asylum in the United States, the asylee will receive a Form I-94/Form I-94A with a stamp or notation indicating asylee status, such as "asylum granted indefinitely" or the appropriate provision of law (8 CFR 274a.12(a)(5) or INA 208). This document is considered a List C document that demonstrates employment authorization in the United States and does not expire. If the asylee chooses to present this document, he or she also will need to present a List B identity document, such as a State-issued driver's license or identification card.

USCIS also issues asylees Employment Authorization Documents (Forms I-766), which are acceptable as List A documents. In some situations, USCIS issues asylees Employment Authorization Documents (Forms I-766) automatically. In other situations, USCIS issues asylees Employment Authorization Documents (Forms I-766) upon request based on the filing of an employment authorization application.

Temporary Protected Status (TPS)

Temporary Protected Status (TPS) is a temporary immigration benefit that allows qualified individuals from designated countries (or parts of those countries) who are in the United States to stay here for a limited time period. As a TPS beneficiary, an employee may choose to present an Employment Authorization Document (Form I-766) to demonstrate employment authorization or any other applicable document or combination of documents

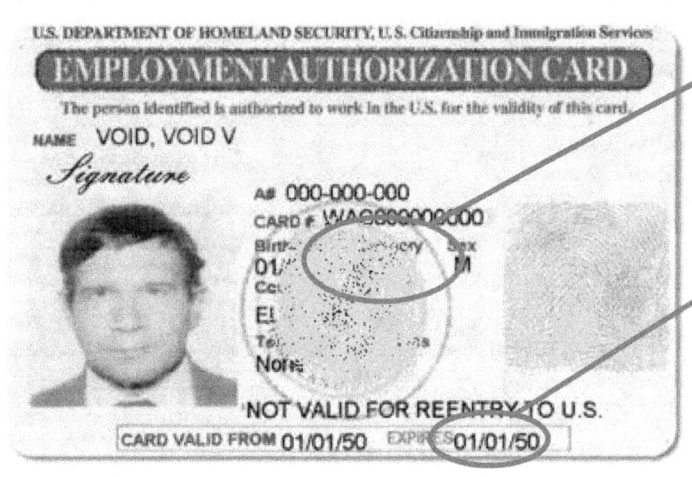

The notation "A-12" or "C-19" appears on the face of the Employment Authorization Document (Form I-766) under "Category."

The expiration date of the last re-registration period appears on the face of the card. (This date will be indicated in the Federal Register notice and may also be found on www.uscis.gov/tps.)

listed on Form I-9 as proof of identity and employment authorization. TPS-related Employment Authorization Documents (Forms I-766) contain an expiration date on their face, but a TPS beneficiary may continue to work after the expiration date if DHS has temporarily extended the validity date of the Employment Authorization Document (Form I-766) through an appropriate notice published in the Federal Register.

When DHS extends a specific TPS country designation, it sometimes issues a Federal Register notice containing a temporary blanket automatic extension of expiring Employment Authorization Documents (Forms I-766) for TPS beneficiaries from that country to allow time for USCIS to issue new Employment Authorization Documents (Forms I-766) bearing updated validity dates. The USCIS website and Federal Register will note if Employment Authorization Documents (Forms I-766) have been automatically extended for TPS beneficiaries from the particular country and to what date. The automatic extension is typically for six months, but the time period can vary. TPS beneficiaries must re-register and, if they request, obtain new Employment Authorization Documents (Forms I-766) before the automatic extension expires.

You may accept an expired Employment Authorization Document (Form I-766) that has been auto-extended to complete the Form I-9, provided the following information appears on the card as shown in the box at the top of the page.

Employers should enter the document name, number, and expiration date in Section 2 under List A, noting the end of the auto-extension period. If an existing employee's EAD has been extended, draw a line through the expiration date for the EAD entered in Section 2; write

the new date to which the EAD has been extended above the previous date; write "EAD Ext." in the margin of Section 2 and initial and date the correction. You may not request that an employee provide proof that he or she is a national of a country that has been designated for TPS. If your employee presents an Employment Authorization Document (Form I-766), you must accept it if it reasonably appears on its face to be genuine and to relate to the employee presenting it.

When the automatic extension of the Employment Authorization Document (Form I-766) expires, you must reverify the employee's employment authorization by entering the document name, number and expiration date in Section 3 of Form I-9 or a new Form I-9, if necessary. The TPS beneficiary may choose to present an unexpired Employment Authorization Document (Form I-766) with an updated expiration date or any other document from List A or C of Form I-9 establishing that he or she continues to be authorized to work in the United States. If the employee presents a renewed Employment Authorization Document (Form I-766), it will bear the notation "A-12" or "C-19" on the face of the card under "Category," and is acceptable under List A as evidence of both identity and employment authorization.

Exchange Visitors and Students

Each year thousands of exchange visitors, international students, and their dependents come to the United States to study and work.

Exchange Visitors (J-1s)

The Department of State administers the exchange visitor program and designates exchange visitor program sponsors. Responsible officers within the program issue Form DS-2019, Certificate of Eligibility for Exchange Visitor

(J-1) Status. Exchange visitors come to the United States for a specific period of time to participate in a particular program or activity, as described on their Form DS-2019. Only J-1 exchange visitors may use Form DS-2019 for employment when such employment is part of their program. Currently, the Department of State designates public and private entities to act as exchange sponsors for the following programs:

Table 2: Exchange Visitor Programs

EXCHANGE VISITOR PROGRAMS
SECONDARY STUDENT
ASSOCIATE DEGREE STUDENT
BACHELOR'S DEGREE STUDENT
MASTER'S DEGREE STUDENT
DOCTORAL STUDENT
NON-DEGREE STUDENT
STUDENT INTERN
TRAINEE (SPECIALTY)
TRAINEE (NON-SPECIALTY)
TEACHER
PROFESSOR
INTERNATIONAL VISITOR
ALIEN PHYSICIAN
GOVERNMENT VISITOR
RESEARCH SCHOLAR
SHORT-TERM SCHOLAR
SPECIALIST
CAMP COUNSELOR
SUMMER WORK/TRAVEL
AU PAIR
TRAINEE
INTERN
Pilot Programs
Summer work/travel: Australia
Summer work/travel: New Zealand
Intern work/travel: Ireland
Work/English Study/travel: South Korea

High school or secondary school students and international visitors are not authorized to work.

Other J-1 students may be authorized by their responsible officer for part-time on-campus employment pursuant to the terms of a scholarship, fellowship, or assistantship or off-campus employment based on serious, urgent, unforeseen economic circumstances as authorized the responsible officer of the school. J-1 students may also be authorized for a maximum of 18 months (or, for Ph.D. students, a maximum of 36 months) of practical training during or immediately after their studies. J-1 practical training includes paid off-campus employment and/or unpaid internships that are part of a J-1 student's program of study. The J-1 student's responsible officer must authorize employment in writing for practical training. Special rules apply to student interns.

Employment for other J-1 exchange visitors is sometimes job- and site-specific or limited to a few months.

For more information about these categories and their employment authorization, please contact the responsible officer whose name and telephone number are on Form DS-2019 or the U.S. Department of State's website at www.exchanges.state.gov.

USCIS does not issue Employment Authorization Documents (Forms I-766) to J-1 exchange visitors. However, they are issued several other documents that, when presented in combination, are acceptable under List A of Form I-9: unexpired foreign passport, Form I-94/Form I-94A and Form DS-2019. If the employee presents this combination of documents when completing Form I-9, ensure that he or she enters his or her admission number from Form I-94/ I-94A in Section 1.

You should enter in Section 2 (or Section 3 if reverifying) under List A the exchange visitor's:

- Unexpired foreign passport number, issuing authority, and passport expiration date,

- 11-digit Form I-94/Form I-94A number and its expiration date (including duration of status, which is indicated on the card as "D/S"), and the

- Form DS-2019 number (SEVIS number) and expiration date of employment authorization listed on the form.

Some exchange visitors may extend their status. If you have questions about any exchange visitor's continued employment authorization, contact the responsible officer whose name and telephone number are on Form DS-2019.

Dependents of a J-1 exchange visitor are classified as J-2 nonimmigrants and are only authorized to work if USCIS has issued them an Employment Authorization Document (Form I-766). A J-2 nonimmigrant's foreign passport and Form I-94/Form I-94A are not evidence of identity and employment authorization for purposes of Form I-9.

F-1 and M-1 Nonimmigrant Students

Foreign students pursuing academic studies and/or language training programs are classified as F-1 nonimmigrants, while foreign students pursuing nonacademic or vocational studies are classified as M-1 nonimmigrants. Designated school officials at certified schools issue Form I-20, *Certificate of Eligibility for Nonimmigrant (F-1)/(M-1) Students.*

F-1 nonimmigrant foreign students may be eligible to work under certain conditions. There are several types of employment authorization for students, including:

1. On-campus employment,

2. Curricular practical training,

3. Off-campus employment based on severe economic hardship,

4. Employment sponsored by an international organization, and

5. Optional practical training (OPT).

On-campus employment does not require designated school official or DHS approval but is limited to 20 hours a week when school is in session. On-campus employment must be performed on the school's premises (including on-location commercial firms that provide services for students on campus, such as the school bookstore or cafeteria), or at an off-campus location that is educationally affiliated with the school. Employment with on-site commercial firms, such as a construction company that builds a school building, is not deemed on-campus employment if it does not provide direct student services. For more information about on-campus employment, you should contact the Student and Exchange Visitor Program (SEVP) at www.ice.gov. The

F-1 student's unexpired foreign passport in combination with his or her Form I-94/Form I-94A indicating F-1 nonimmigrant status would qualify as a List A document for Form I-9 purposes.

Curricular practical training allows students to accept paid alternative work/study, internship, cooperative education, or any other type of required internship or practicum that is offered by sponsoring employers through cooperative agreements with the school. The curricular practical training program must be an integral part of the curriculum of the student's degree program. The designated school official must authorize curricular practical training. The following documents establish the student's identity and employment authorization for Form I-9 purposes and should be entered in Section 2 under List A of Form I-9:

- The student's foreign passport;

- Form I-20 with the designated school official's endorsement for employment on page 3; and

- A valid Form I-94/Form I-94A indicating F-1 nonimmigrant status.

Ensure that the student enters his or her admission number from Form I-94/Form I-94A in Section 1.

For the other types of employment available to eligible foreign students, employment authorization must be granted by USCIS, and will be evidenced by an Employment Authorization Document (Form I-766) issued by USCIS.

Border commuter students who enter the United States with an F-1 visa may only work as part of their curricular practical training or post-completion practical training.

M-1 students may only accept employment if it is part of a practical training program after completion of their course of study. USCIS will issue the Employment Authorization Document (Form I-766) with authorization granted for a maximum period of six months of full-time practical training, depending on the length of the students' full-time study.

The dependents of F-1 and M-1 foreign students will have an F-2 or M-2 visa and are not eligible for employment authorization.

Section 1. Employee Information and Attestation (*Employees must complete and sign Section 1 of Form I-9 no later than the **first day of employment**, but not before accepting a job offer.*)

Last Name (*Family Name*)	First Name (*Given Name*)	Middle Initial	Other Names Used (*if any*)
Tres	Michelle	S	N/A

Address (*Street Number and Name*)	Apt. Number	City or Town	State	Zip Code
789 N. Main Street	2B	Collegeville	MD	12345

Date of Birth (*mm/dd/yyyy*)	U.S. Social Security Number	E-mail Address	Telephone Number
07/21/1994	0 0 0 - 0 0 - 0 0 0 0	michelletres@email.com	(301) 123-4567

I am aware that federal law provides for imprisonment and/or fines for false statements or use of false documents in connection with the completion of this form.

I attest, under penalty of perjury, that I am (check one of the following):

☐ A citizen of the United States

☐ A noncitizen national of the United States (*See instructions*)

☐ A lawful permanent resident (Alien Registration Number/USCIS Number): _____

☒ An alien authorized to work until (expiration date, if applicable, mm/dd/yyyy) _D/S_____ . Some aliens may write "N/A" in this field. (*See instructions*)

For aliens authorized to work, provide your Alien Registration Number/USCIS Number **OR** Form I-94 Admission Number:

1. Alien Registration Number/USCIS Number: _____

OR

2. Form I-94 Admission Number: _0 0 0 0 0 0 0 0 0 0 0_

If you obtained your admission number from CBP in connection with your arrival in the United States, include the following:

Foreign Passport Number: _#00XX00000_

Country of Issuance: _France_

Some aliens may write "N/A" on the Foreign Passport Number and Country of Issuance fields. (*See instructions*)

3-D Barcode		
Do Not Write in This Space		

Signature of Employee: *Michelle S. Tres*   Date (*mm/dd/yyyy*): 06/30/2013

Figure 7: Completing Section 1 of Form I-9 for Students in Curricular Practical Training

① Student completes Section 1 and enters his or her 11-digit Form I-94/Form I-94A number.

② Student signs and dates the form.

Section 2. Employer or Authorized Representative Review and Verification

(Employers or their authorized representative must complete and sign Section 2 within 3 business days of the employee's first day of employment. You must physically examine one document from List A OR examine a combination of one document from List B and one document from List C as listed on the "Lists of Acceptable Documents" on the next page of this form. For each document you review, record the following information: document title, issuing authority, document number, and expiration date, if any.)

(1) Employee Last Name, First Name and Middle Initial from Section 1: Tres, Michelle S

List A Identity and Employment Authorization	OR	List B Identity	AND	List C Employment Authorization
(2) Document Title: French Passport		Document Title:		Document Title:
Issuing Authority: France		Issuing Authority:		Issuing Authority:
Document Number: #00XX00000		Document Number:		Document Number:
Expiration Date *(if any)(mm/dd/yyyy)*: 05/13/2020		Expiration Date *(if any)(mm/dd/yyyy)*:		Expiration Date *(if any)(mm/dd/yyyy)*:
Document Title: I-94				
Issuing Authority: DHS				
Document Number: 00000000000				
Expiration Date *(if any)(mm/dd/yyyy)*: D/S				
Document Title: Form I-20				3-D Barcode Do Not Write in This Space
Issuing Authority: DHS				
Document Number: N0000000000				
Expiration Date *(if any)(mm/dd/yyyy)*: 06/30/2015				

Certification

I attest, under penalty of perjury, that (1) I have examined the document(s) presented by the above-named employee, (2) the above-listed document(s) appear to be genuine and to relate to the employee named, and (3) to the best of my knowledge the employee is authorized to work in the United States.

(3) The employee's first day of employment *(mm/dd/yyyy)*: 06/30/2013 *(See instructions for exemptions.)*

(4) Signature of Employer or Authorized Representative Timothy Hardy	Date *(mm/dd/yyyy)* 07/01/2013	Title of Employer or Authorized Representative Store Manager
Last Name *(Family Name)* Hardy	First Name *(Given Name)* Timothy	Employer's Business or Organization Name Campus Bookstore

(5) Employer's Business or Organization Address *(Street Number and Name)* 456 Campus Way	City or Town Collegeville	State MD	Zip Code 12345

Figure 8: Completing Section 2 of Form I-9 for Students in Curricular Practical Training

(1) Enter the student's name from Section 1 at the top of Section 2.

(2) Enter the student's foreign passport number, Form I-94/Form I-94A and Form I-20 that specifies that you are his or her approved employer as shown.

(3) Enter the date employment began.

(4) Employer or authorized representative attests to physically examining the documents provided by signing and dating the signature and date fields.

(5) Enter the business name and address.

Optional Practical Training (OPT) for F-1 Students— EAD required

OPT provides practical experience in an F-1 academic student's major area of study. An F-1 academic student may engage in OPT while studying and may work up to 20 hours per week while school is in session and full-time (20 or more hours per week) when school is not in session. After completing their course of study, students also may engage in OPT for work experience. USCIS may authorize an F-1 academic student to have up to 12 months of OPT upon completion of his or her degree program. Some F-1 students may be eligible for an extension of their OPT, as described below.

The designated school official must update Form I-20 to show that he or she has recommended OPT and to show the date employment can begin. OPT employment must be directly related to the student's field of study noted on Form I-20. The student cannot begin OPT until USCIS has granted his or her application for employment authorization.

(1)

Section 1. Employee Information and Attestation *(Employees must complete and sign Section 1 of Form I-9 no later than the **first day of employment**, but not before accepting a job offer.)*

Last Name *(Family Name)*	First Name *(Given Name)*	Middle Initial	Other Names Used *(if any)*
Louis	Paul	W	N/A

Address *(Street Number and Name)*	Apt. Number	City or Town	State	Zip Code
123 University Street	F	Collegeville	MD	12345

Date of Birth *(mm/dd/yyyy)*	U.S. Social Security Number	E-mail Address	Telephone Number
03/02/1994	0 0 0 - 0 0 - 0 0 0 0	paullouis@email.com	(301) 765-4321

I am aware that federal law provides for imprisonment and/or fines for false statements or use of false documents in connection with the completion of this form.

I attest, under penalty of perjury, that I am (check one of the following):

☐ A citizen of the United States

☐ A noncitizen national of the United States *(See instructions)*

☐ A lawful permanent resident (Alien Registration Number/USCIS Number): _____

☒ An alien authorized to work until (expiration date, if applicable, mm/dd/yyyy) 08/31/2015 . Some aliens may write "N/A" in this field. *(See instructions)*

For aliens authorized to work, provide your Alien Registration Number/USCIS Number **OR** Form I-94 Admission Number:

1. Alien Registration Number/USCIS Number: 1 2 3 4 5 6 7 8 9

OR

2. Form I-94 Admission Number: _____

3-D Barcode
Do Not Write in This Space

If you obtained your admission number from CBP in connection with your arrival in the United States, include the following:

Foreign Passport Number: _____

Country of Issuance: _____

Some aliens may write "N/A" on the Foreign Passport Number and Country of Issuance fields. *(See instructions)*

(2)

Signature of Employee: *Paul W. Louis*	Date *(mm/dd/yyyy)*: 06/30/2013

Figure 9: Completing Section 1 of Form I-9 for F-1 Nonimmigrant Students with OPT

(1) F-1 nonimmigrant student completes Section 1.

(2) Student signs and dates the form.

Section 2. Employer or Authorized Representative Review and Verification

(Employers or their authorized representative must complete and sign Section 2 within 3 business days of the employee's first day of employment. You must physically examine one document from List A OR examine a combination of one document from List B and one document from List C as listed on the "Lists of Acceptable Documents" on the next page of this form. For each document you review, record the following information: document title, issuing authority, document number, and expiration date, if any.)

① Employee Last Name, First Name and Middle Initial from Section 1: Louis, Paul W

List A Identity and Employment Authorization	**OR**	**List B** Identity	**AND**	**List C** Employment Authorization
Document Title: EAD		Document Title:		Document Title:
Issuing Authority: DHS		Issuing Authority:		Issuing Authority:
Document Number: XXX000000000		Document Number:		Document Number:
Expiration Date *(if any)(mm/dd/yyyy)*: 08/31/2015		Expiration Date *(if any)(mm/dd/yyyy)*:		Expiration Date *(if any)(mm/dd/yyyy)*:
Document Title:				
Issuing Authority:				
Document Number:				
Expiration Date *(if any)(mm/dd/yyyy)*:				
Document Title:				
Issuing Authority:				
Document Number:				
Expiration Date *(if any)(mm/dd/yyyy)*:				3-D Barcode Do Not Write in This Space

② (List A column)

Certification

I attest, under penalty of perjury, that (1) I have examined the document(s) presented by the above-named employee, (2) the above-listed document(s) appear to be genuine and to relate to the employee named, and (3) to the best of my knowledge the employee is authorized to work in the United States.

③ The employee's first day of employment *(mm/dd/yyyy)*: 06/30/2013   **(See instructions for exemptions.)**

Signature of Employer or Authorized Representative *Timothy Hardy*	Date *(mm/dd/yyyy)* 06/30/2013	Title of Employer or Authorized Representative Project Manager
Last Name *(Family Name)* Hardy	First Name *(Given Name)* Timothy	Employer's Business or Organization Name Computer Technology, Inc.

④ (Signature row)

Employer's Business or Organization Address *(Street Number and Name)* 456 Linux Avenue	City or Town Windowsville	State MD	Zip Code 12345

⑤ (Address row)

Figure 10: Completing Section 2 of Form I-9 for F-1 Nonimmigrant Students with OPT

① Enter the student's name from Section 1 at the top of Section 2.

② Enter the student's Employment Authorization Document (Form I-766) as shown.

③ Enter date employment began.

④ Employer or authorized representative attests to physically examining the documents provided by signing and dating the signature and date fields.

⑤ Enter the business name and address.

F-1 OPT STEM Extension

An F-1 academic student who received a bachelor's, master's, or doctoral degree in science, technology, engineering, or mathematics (STEM) may apply for a one-time 17-month extension of his or her OPT. To qualify, a student must have completed a degree included in the DHS STEM Designated Degree Program List found on ICE's website at www.ice.gov/sevis/stemlist.htm. You must be enrolled in E-Verify in good standing and provide your E-Verify company identification number to the student for the student to apply to USCIS for the STEM extension using Form I-765, *Application for Employment Authorization*. A STEM student may change employers, but the new employer must be enrolled in E-Verify before the student begins work for pay.

If the student's Employment Authorization Document (Form I-766) expires while his or her STEM extension application is pending, he or she is authorized to work until USCIS makes a decision on his or her application, but not more than 180 days from the date the student's initial OPT Employment Authorization Document (Form I-766) expires.

The student's expired Employment Authorization Document (Form I-766), together with his or her Form I-20 endorsed by the designated school official recommending the STEM extension are acceptable proof of identity and employment authorization for Form I-9 purposes. Enter these documents in Section 2 under List A of Form I-9. You should reverify employment authorization no later than 180 days from the expiration date of the previous Employment Authorization Document (Form I-766).

Cap-Gap

F-1 students who seek to change to H-1B status may be eligible for a cap-gap extension of status and employment authorization through September 30 of the calendar year for which the H-1B petition is being filed, but only if the H-1B status will begin on October 1. The term cap-gap refers to the period between the time a nonimmigrant's F-1 student status would ordinarily end and his or her H-1B status begins. If you employ an F-1 nonimmigrant student in OPT and you filed an H-1B petition for that student, he or she may be able to continue working beyond the expiration date on his or her OPT Employment Authorization Document (Form I-766) while the petition is pending.

There are two types of cap-gap extensions:

1. Extensions of status only.

If a student is in F-1 status when you file an H-1B petition with an October 1 start date, but the student is not currently participating in OPT, the student will receive a cap-gap extension of his or her F-1 status, but will not be authorized to work until USCIS approves the H-1B petition and the H-1B status begins on October 1.

2. Extensions of F-1 status and OPT.

If a student is in F-1 status when you file an H-1B petition with an October 1 start date and the student is currently participating in post-completion OPT, the student will receive an automatic cap-gap extension of both his or her F-1 student status and his or her authorized period of post-completion OPT. If the H-1B petition is selected and approved, the student will remain authorized to work as an F-1 student with OPT through September 30.

The student's expired OPT Employment Authorization Document (Form I-766), along with Form I-20, which shows that the cap-gap extension was endorsed by the student's designated school official, would qualify as a List A document. You should enter these documents in Section 2 under List A (or Section 3 if reverifying) of Form I-9. These documents are acceptable for establishing employment authorization through September 30 of the year in which you filed the H-1B petition or until the H-1B petition is rejected, denied, or withdrawn. You must reverify employment authorization when the Form I-20 cap-gap endorsement expires but not later than October 1.

H-1B Specialty Occupations

U.S. businesses use the H-1B program to temporarily employ foreign workers in a specialty occupation that requires theoretical or technical expertise in a certain field, such as science, engineering or computer programming. As a U.S. employer, you may submit a Form I-129, *Petition for a Nonimmigrant Worker*, to USCIS for nonimmigrants who have certain skills, provided those individuals meet established requirements. You must also include an approved Form ETA 9035, *Labor Certification Application*, with Form I-129.

A newly hired employee with H-1B classification

If USCIS approves your petition, you will receive Form I-797, Notice of Approval, from USCIS, which indicates that the foreign worker has been approved for H-1B status. Once your employee begins working for you, you must complete a Form I-9 for this employee.

H-1B continuing employment with the same employer

For an H-1B worker to continue working for you beyond the expiration of his or her current H-1B status, indicated by the expiration date on his or her Form I-94/Form I-94A, you must request an extension of stay before his or her H-1B status expires. Upon submitting a timely filed Form I-129 petition seeking an extension of the employee's status to USCIS, the employee is authorized to continue to work while the petition is being processed for a period not to exceed 240 days, or until USCIS denies your petition, whichever comes first. Write "240-Day Ext." and enter the date you submitted Form I-129 to USCIS in the margin of Form I-9 next to Section 2. You must reverify the employee's employment authorization in Section 3 once you receive a decision on the H-1B petition or by the end of the 240-day period, whichever comes first.

See *Completing Form I-9 for Nonimmigrant Categories when Requesting Extensions of Stay* below.

H-1B employees changing employers (porting)

Under the American Competitiveness Act in the Twenty-First Century (AC-21), an H-1B employee who is changing employers within the H-1B program may begin working for you as soon as you file a Form I-129 petition on his or her behalf. To qualify for AC-21 benefits, the new petition must not be frivolous and must have been filed prior to the expiration of the individual's period of authorized stay. You must complete a new Form I-9 for this newly hired employee. An H-1B employee's Form I-94/Form I-94A issued for employment with the previous employer, along with his or her foreign passport, would qualify as a List A document. You should write "AC-21" and enter the date you submitted Form I-129 to USCIS in the margin of Form I-9 next to Section 2.

See *Completing Form I-9 for Nonimmigrant Categories when Requesting Extensions of Stay* below.

For more information about employing H-1B workers, please visit www.uscis.gov.

H-2A Temporary Agricultural Worker Program

The H-2A program allows U.S. employers to bring foreign workers to the United States to fill temporary or seasonal agricultural jobs, usually lasting no longer than one year, for which U.S. workers are not available. Before filing a petition with USCIS, you must first obtain a valid temporary labor certification for H-2A workers from the U.S. Department of Labor (DOL). Once certified, you can include multiple workers when filing a Form I-129 peti-tion requesting H-2A classification from USCIS. If USCIS approves your petition, you can hire the foreign workers for which you petitioned to fill the temporary job.

A newly hired employee in H-2A classification

Complete a new Form I-9 for this employee as you would for any employee. An H-2A worker's unexpired Form I-94/Form I-94A indicating his or her H-2A status, along with his or her foreign passport, would qualify as a List A document. Enter these documents in Section 2 under List A, along with the expiration date of your employee's H-2A status found on his or her Form I-94/Form I-94A.

H-2A continuing employment with the same employer

You may extend your worker's H-2A status in increments of no longer than one year by timely filing with USCIS a new Form I-129 petition on behalf of the worker. Please note that in most cases, a new temporary labor certification from DOL is required to qualify for an extension of H-2A employment. You must acquire this certification, if required, before you can file Form I-129. To avoid disruption of employment, you should file a petition to extend the employee's employment authorization status well before it expires. Write "240-Day Ext." and enter the date you submitted Form I-129 to USCIS in the margin of Form I-9 next to Section 2. USCIS may extend a single H-2A petition for up to two weeks without an additional approved labor certification under certain circumstances. In such a case, write "two-week extension" and enter the date you submitted Form I-129 to USCIS in the margin of Form I-9.

Upon submitting a new Form I-129 petition to USCIS, the H-2A worker is authorized to continue to work while the petition is being processed for a period not to exceed 240 days, or until USCIS denies your petition, whichever comes first. You must reverify the employee's employment authorization in Section 3 once you receive a decision on the H-2A petition or by the end of the 240-day period, whichever comes first.

See *Completing Form I-9 for Nonimmigrant Categories when Requesting Extensions of Stay* below.

H-2A extension with a new employer (porting)

In most cases, an H-2A worker may not begin working for a new employer until USCIS approves the petition requesting a change of employer. However, if you participate in E-Verify, you may employ an H-2A worker as soon as you submit a new Form I-129 petition on his or her behalf. The porting H-2A worker is authorized to work while USCIS processes the petition for a period not to exceed 120 days, or until USCIS denies your petition, whichever comes first. Your newly hired employee must complete Form I-9. The H-2A employee's unexpired Form I-94/Form I-94A indicating his or her H-2A status, along with his or her foreign passport, would qualify as a List A document. You should write "120-Day Ext." and enter the date you submitted Form I-129 to USCIS in the margin of Form I-9 next to Section 2.

If USCIS denies the new petition before the 120-day period expires, USCIS will automatically terminate the H-2A worker's employment authorization within 15 calendar days of its denial decision. USCIS may also terminate employment authorization if you fail to remain an E-Verify participant in good standing. You must reverify the employee's employment authorization in Section 3 either by the end of the 120-day period or once you receive a decision on the H-2A petition, whichever is earlier. If your petition is denied, count 15 days from the date of the denial for the date when the employee's employment authorization expires.

See *Completing Form I-9 for Nonimmigrant Categories when Requesting Extensions of Stay* below.

For more information about employing H-2A workers, please visit www.uscis.gov.

Extensions of Stay for Other Nonimmigrant Categories

Other nonimmigrants also may receive extensions of stay on their nonimmigrant status with the same employer if the employer files a Form I-129 petition with USCIS on their behalf before the nonimmigrant's current immigration status expires. These employees are authorized to continue to work while the petition is being processed for a period not to exceed 240 days, or until USCIS denies your petition, whichever comes first. You should write "240-day Ext." and the date you submitted Form I-129 to USCIS in the margin of Form I-9 next to Section 2.

Other categories include: E-1, E-2, H-2B, H-3, L-1, O-1, O-2, P-1, P-2, P-3, R-1 and TN (per 8 CFR 274a.12 (b) (20)). Note that individuals in the E-1 and E-2 categories are employers.

Please go to www.uscis.gov/files/form/i-129instr.pdf for further instructions on filing extensions of stay.

See *Completing Form I-9 for Nonimmigrant Categories when Requesting Extensions of Stay* below.

For more information about employing other types of nonimmigrant workers, please visit www.uscis.gov.

Completing Form I-9 for Nonimmigrant Categories when Requesting Extensions of Stay

You must submit a timely filed Form I-129 petition to USCIS to request an extension of stay on behalf of an employee in one of the above categories. While the petition is pending, your existing employee is authorized to continue to work for you, for 120 days to 240 days, depending on the category petitioned for, or until USCIS denies your petition, whichever comes first.

You should retain the following documents with the employee's existing Form I-9 to show that you filed for an extension of stay on the employee's behalf:

* A copy of the new Form I-129;

* Proof of payment for filing a new Form I-129; and

* Evidence that you mailed the new Form I-129 to USCIS.

After submitting Form I-129 to USCIS, you will receive a notice from USCIS acknowledging that your petition is pending, which you should retain with the employee's Form I-9.

If USCIS approves the application/petition for an extension of stay, you will receive a Form I-797(A), which includes an expiration date and an attached Form I-94A, Arrival/Departure Record. Enter the document title, number and expiration date listed on the notice in Section 3 of Form I-9. You must give your employee the Form I-94A, which is evidence of his or her employment-authorized nonimmigrant status.

Completing Section 3

Recording Changes of Name and Other Identity Information for Current Employees

In the case of a rehire or reverification, if an employee has had a legal change of name, such as following marriage, you must record the employee's legal change of name in the space provided in Section 3 of Form I-9. If you learn of a legal change of name at a time other than during a rehire or reverification, USCIS recommends that you update Form I-9 with the new name in the space provided in Section 3 of Form I-9 so that you maintain correct information on the form. In either situation, you should take steps to be reasonably assured of the employee's identity and the veracity of the employee's claim of a legal name change. These steps may include asking the employee for the reason for the legal change of name and to provide documentation of a legal change of name to keep with Form I-9, so that your actions are well-documented if the government asks to inspect your Forms I-9.

You may encounter situations other than a legal change of name where an employee informs you or you have reason to believe that his or her identity is different from that previously used to complete the Form I-9. For example, an employee may have been working under a false identity, has subsequently obtained a work authorized immigration status in his or her true identity, and wishes to regularize his or her employment records. In that circumstance you should complete a new Form I-9. Write the original hire date in Section 2, and attach the new Form I-9 to the previously completed Form I-9 and include a written explanation.

In cases where an employee has worked for you using a false identity but is currently work authorized, the I-9 rules do not require termination of employment. However, there may be other laws, contractual obligations, or company policies that you should consider prior to taking action.

For E-Verify employers:

- USCIS recommends that you encourage your employees to record their legal name change with the Social Security Administration to avoid mismatches in E-Verify.

- If you complete a new Form I-9 in a new identity situation as described above, e.g., where a name change to Form I-9 information is not a legal name change, you should verify the new Form I-9 information through E-Verify. If you do not complete a new Form I-9, you should not begin a new E-Verify case.

- Federal contractors who are subject to the FAR E-Verify clause and who choose to verify existing employees by updating existing Forms I-9 have special rules pertaining to when they must complete new Forms I-9. Under this option, a new Form I-9 must be completed when an employee changes his or her name. For more information, see the E-Verify Supplemental Guide for Federal Contractors, available at www.dhs.gov/E-Verify.

Reverifying or Updating Employment Authorization for Rehired Employees

If you rehire an employee within three years of the date of the initial execution of his or her previous Form I-9,

you may complete a new Form I-9 or you may be able to rely on the previously completed Form I-9 in certain circumstances.

Inspect the previously completed Form I-9 and:

1. If the employee's previously completed Form I-9 indicates that the individual is still eligible to work, you are not required to complete a new Form I-9 but may rely on the previously completed Form I-9 to meet the verification requirements for this employee. You must update the previously completed Form I-9 in Block B in Section 3 with the date of rehire.

OR

2. If you determine that the employee's employment authorization has expired, you must reverify employment authorization in Block C of Section 3 of the previously completed Form I-9, or use page 2 of a new Form I-9 if Section 3 has already been used.

To reverify:

1. Enter the date of rehire in Block B of Section 3.

2. Enter the document title, number, and expiration date (if any) of the document(s) the employee presents in Block C of Section 3.

3. Sign and date Section 3.

4. If you choose to use a new Form I-9, enter the employee's name at the top of page 2 of a new Form I-9 and complete Section 3 of the new Form I-9, retaining the new form with the previously completed one.

5. You must reverify the employee on a new Form I-9 if the version of the form you used for the previous verification is no longer valid. Please check www.uscis.gov/I-9 for currently valid Form(s) I-9.

To update (optional), you must:

1. Enter the date of rehire in Block B and the employee's new name, if applicable, in Block A of Section 3.

2. Sign and date Section 3.

3. If you are updating on a new Form I-9, enter the employee's name at the top of page 2 and use Section 3 of the new Form I-9 to update, retaining the new Form I-9 with the previously completed Form I-9.

Section 3. Reverification and Rehires (To be completed and signed by employer or authorized representative.)			
A. New Name (if applicable) Last Name (Family Name) First Name (Given Name)		Middle Initial	B. Date of Rehire (if applicable) (mm/dd/yyyy):
Doe	Jason	A	03/28/2015

C. If employee's previous grant of employment authorization has expired, provide the information for the document from List A or List C the employee presented that establishes current employment authorization in the space provided below.

Document Title:	Document Number	Expiration Date (if any)(mm/dd/yyyy):
EAD	XXX1987654321	06/30/2019

I attest, under penalty of perjury, that to the best of my knowledge, this employee is authorized to work in the United States, and if the employee presented document(s), the document(s) I have examined appear to be genuine and to relate to the individual.

Signature of Employer or Authorized Representative:	Date (mm/dd/yyyy):	Print Name of Employer or Authorized Representative:
alice Smith	03/28/2015	Alice Smith

Figure 11: Completing Section 3: Reverification and Rehires

1. Enter the employee's new name, if applicable, in Block A.

2. Enter the employee's date of rehire, if applicable, in Block B.

3. Enter the document title, number, and expiration date (if any) of document(s) presented in Block C.

4. Sign and date Section 3.

Leaves of Absence, Layoffs, Corporate Mergers and Other Interruptions of Employment

You must complete a new Form I-9 when a hire takes place, unless you are rehiring an employee within three years of the date of the initial execution of his or her previous Form I-9. However, in certain situations, a hire is not considered to have taken place despite an interruption in employment. In case of an interruption in employment, you should determine whether the employee is continuing in his or her employment and has a reasonable expectation of employment at all times.

These situations constitute continuing employment:

- Approved paid or unpaid leave on account of study, illness or disability of a family member, illness or pregnancy, maternity or paternity leave, vacation, union business, or other temporary leave approved by the employer.

- Promotions, demotions or pay raises.

- Temporary layoff for lack of work.

- Strikes or labor disputes.

- Reinstatement after disciplinary suspension for wrongful termination found unjustified by any court, arbitrator or administrative body, or otherwise resolved through reinstatement or settlement.

- Transfer from one distinct unit of an employer to another distinct unit of the same employer; the employer may transfer the employee's Form I-9 to the receiving unit.

- Seasonal employment.

- Continuing employment with a related, successor, or reorganized employer, provided that the employer obtains and maintains, from the previous employer, records and Forms I-9 where applicable. A related, successor, or reorganized employer includes:

  - The same employer at another location;

  - An employer who continues to employ any employee of another employer's workforce, where both employers belong to the same multi-employer association and the employee continues to work in the same bargaining unit under the same collective bargaining agreement. For these purposes, any agent designated to complete and maintain Forms I-9 must enter the employee's date of hire and/or termination each time the employee is hired and/or terminated by an employer of the multi-employer association.

NOTE: The related, successor, or reorganized employer may choose to treat these employees as new hires and complete new Forms I-9 for each of them.

To determine whether an employee continuing in his or employment had a reasonable expectation of employment at all times, you should consider several factors, including, but not limited to:

- The individual was employed on a regular and substantial basis. A determination of a regular and substantial basis is established by a comparison of other workers similarly employed by the employer.

- The individual complied with the employer's established and published policy regarding his or her absence.

- The employer's past history of recalling absent employees for employment indicates a likelihood that the individual in question will resume employment with the employer within a reasonable time in the future.

- The former position held by the individual has not been taken permanently by another worker.

- The individual has not sought or obtained benefits during his or her absence from employment with the employer that are inconsistent with an expectation of resuming employment within a reasonable time in the future.

- The financial condition of the employer indicates the ability of the employer to permit the individual in question to resume employment within a reasonable time in the future.

- The oral and/or written communication between employer, the employer's supervisory employees and the individual indicates that it is reasonably

likely that the individual will resume employment within a reasonable time in the future.

Continue to maintain and store the previously completed Form I-9 as if there was no interruption in employment. It is advisable to inspect the previously completed Form I-9 and, if necessary, update the form or conduct reverification.

If you determine that your employee was terminated and is now rehired, and the rehire occurs within three years from the date the original Form I-9 was completed, you may have an option to complete a new Form I-9 or rely on the original Form I-9.

Special Rules for Members of Employer Associations

Special rules apply for employers that are members of an association of two or more employers that have entered into a collective bargaining agreement with one or more employee organizations. An employer that is a member of the employer association will be deemed to have complied with the employment eligibility verification requirements for its employee if:

- The employee is a member of a collective-bargaining unit and is employed, under a collective bargaining agreement between one or more employee organizations and an association of two or more employers, by an employer that is a member of such association, and

- Another employer that is a member of the same employer association (or an agent of the employer association on behalf of the employer), has previously complied with the employment eligibility verification requirements for this individual within three years (or, if less, the period of time that the individual is authorized to be employed in the United States).

Penalties for employing aliens knowing they are unauthorized to work in the United States still apply.

Part Three
Photocopying and Retaining Form I-9

Employers must retain an employee's completed Form I-9 for as long as the individual works for the employer. Once the individual's employment has terminated, the employer must determine how long after termination the Form I-9 must be retained, which is either three years after the date of hire, or one year after the date employment is terminated, whichever is later. Forms I-9 can be retained either on paper or microform, or electronically.

To store Forms I-9 electronically, you may use any electronic recordkeeping, attestation, and retention system that complies with DHS standards, including most commercially available off-the-shelf computer programs and commercial automated data processing systems. However, the system must not be subject to any agreement that would restrict access to and use of it by an agency of the United States. (See *Electronic Retention of Forms I-9* on the next page for additional requirements.)

---

1.   Enter date employee started work: _____

                                                  Add 3 years to Line 1   A. _____

2.   Termination date: _____

                                                  Add 1 year to Line 2   B. _____

             Which date is later: A or B? Enter later date here.   C. _____

                                                          Store Form I-9 until this date.

Figure 8: Form I-9 Retention Calculator

Paper Retention of Forms I-9

Forms I-9 can be signed and stored in paper format with original handwritten signatures. Simply photocopy or print a blank Form I-9. Ensure that the employee receives the instructions for completing the form. When copying or printing the paper Form I-9, you may photocopy the two-sided form by making either double-sided or single-sided copies.

Only the pages of the Form I-9 on which you or the employee enter data must be retained. You may retain completed paper forms on-site or at an off-site storage facility for the required retention period, as long as you are able to present the Forms I-9 within three days of an inspection request from DHS, OSC, or U.S. Department of Labor (DOL) officers.

Microform Retention of Forms I-9

You may retain copies of original signed Forms I-9 on microfilm or microfiche. Only the pages of the Form I-9 on which you or the employee enter data must be retained. To do so, you should:

1. Select film stock that will preserve the image and allow its access and use for the entire retention period, which could be upward of 20 years, depending on the employee and your business.

2. Use well-maintained equipment to create and view microfilms and microfiche that provides clear viewing, and can reproduce legible paper copies. DHS officers must have access to clear, readable documents should they need to inspect your forms.

3. Place indexes either in the first frames of the first roll of film or in the last frames of the last roll of film of a series. For microfiche, place them in the last frames of the last microfiche or microfilm jacket of a series.

Electronic Retention of Forms I-9

USCIS provides a Portable Document Format (.pdf) fillable-printable Form I-9 from its website, www.uscis.gov. In addition, you may generate and retain Form I-9 electronically as long as the employee receives instructions for completing the form and:

1. The resulting form is legible;

2. No change is made to the name, content, or sequence of the data elements and instructions;

3. No additional data elements or language are inserted; and

4. The standards specified in the regulations are met. (8 CFR Part 274a.2(e), (f), (g), (h) and (i) as applicable.)

Employers may use paper, electronic systems, or a combination of paper and electronic systems. You may complete or retain Form I-9 in an electronic generation or storage system that includes:

1. Reasonable controls to ensure the integrity, accuracy and reliability of the electronic generation or storage system;

2. Reasonable controls designed to prevent and detect the unauthorized or accidental creation of, addition to, alteration of, deletion of, or deterioration of an electronically completed or stored Form I-9, including the electronic signature, if used;

3. An inspection and quality assurance program that regularly evaluates the electronic generation or storage system, and includes periodic checks of electronically stored Forms I-9, including the electronic signature, if used;

4. An indexing system that permits the identification and retrieval for viewing or reproducing of relevant documents and records maintained in an electronic storage system; and

5. The ability to reproduce legible and readable paper copies.

If you choose to complete or retain Forms I-9 electronically, you may use one or more electronic generation or storage systems, as long as Forms I-9 retained in the system remain fully accessible and meet the regulations. You may change electronic storage systems as long as the systems meet the performance requirement of the regulations. For each electronic generation or storage system used, you must maintain and make available upon request complete descriptions of:

1. The electronic generation and storage system, including all procedures relating to its use.

2. The indexing system that permits the identification and retrieval of relevant documents and records maintained in an electronic storage system. You are not required to maintain separate indexing databases for each system if comparable results can be achieved without separate indexing databases.

Only the pages of the Form I-9 on which you or the employee enter data must be retained.

NOTE: Forms I-9 must be stored for three years after the date you hire an employee, or one year after the employee's employment ends, whichever is later, which can result in a long retention period. For example, if an employee retires from your company after 15 years, you will need to store his or her Form I-9 for a total of 16 years.

Documentation of Electronic Storage Systems

If you choose to complete or retain Forms I-9 electronically, you must maintain and make available upon request documentation of the business processes that:

1. Create the retained Forms I-9,

2. Modify and maintain the retained Forms I-9, and

3. Establish the authenticity and integrity of the forms, such as audit trails.

NOTE: Insufficient or incomplete documentation is a violation of section 274A(a)(1)(B) of the INA (8 CFR Part 274a.2(f)(2)).

Electronic Signature of Forms I-9

You may choose to fill out a paper Form I-9 and scan and upload the original signed form to retain it electronically. Once you have securely stored Form I-9 in electronic format, you may destroy the original paper Form I-9.

If you complete Forms I-9 electronically using an electronic signature, your system for capturing electronic signatures must allow signatories to acknowledge that they read the attestation and attach the electronic signature to an electronically completed Form I-9. The system must also:

1. Affix the electronic signature at the time of the transaction;

2. Create and preserve a record verifying the identity of the person producing the signature; and

3. Upon request of the employee, provide a printed confirmation of the transaction to the person providing the signature.

Employers who complete Forms I-9 electronically must attest to the required information in Section 2 of Form I-9. The system used to capture the electronic signature should include a method to acknowledge that the attestation to be signed has been read by the signatory.

NOTE: If you choose to use an electronic signature to complete Form I-9, but do not comply with these standards, DHS will determine that you have not properly completed Form I-9, in violation of section 274A(a)(1)(B) of the INA (8 CFR Part 274a.2(b)(2)).

Security

If you retain Forms I-9 electronically, you must implement an effective records security program that:

1. Ensures that only authorized personnel have access to electronic records;

2. Provides for backup and recovery of records to protect against information loss;

3. Ensures that employees are trained to minimize the risk of unauthorized or accidental alteration or erasure of electronic records; and

4. Ensures that whenever an individual creates, completes, updates, modifies, alters, or corrects an electronic record, the system creates a secure and permanent record that establishes the date of access, the identity of the individual who accessed the electronic record, and the particular action taken.

NOTE: If an employer's action or inaction results in the alteration, loss, or erasure of electronic records, and the employer knew, or reasonably should have known, that the action or inaction could have that effect, the employer is in violation of section 274A(b)(3) of the INA (8 CFR Part 274a.2(g)(2)).

Retaining Copies of Form I-9 Documentation

You may choose to copy or scan documents an employee presents when completing Form I-9, which you may, but are not required to, retain with his or her Form I-9. Even if you retain copies of documentation, you are still required to fully complete Section 2 of Form I-9. If you choose to retain copies of an employee's documents, you must do so for all employees, regardless of national origin or citizenship status, or you may be in violation of anti-discrimination laws.

Copies or electronic images of presented documents must be retrievable consistent with DHS's standards on electronic retention, documentation, security, and electronic signatures for employers and employees, as specified in 8 CFR Part 274a.2(b)(3).

If copies or electronic images of the employee's documents are made, they must either be retained with Form I-9 or stored with the employee's records.

Inspection

The Immigration and Nationality Act (INA) specifically authorizes DHS, OSC, and DOL to inspect Forms I-9. DHS, OSC, and DOL provide employers a minimum of three days' notice prior to inspecting retained Forms I-9. The employer must make Forms I-9 available upon request at the location where DHS, OSC, or DOL requests to see them.

If you store Forms I-9 at an off-site location, inform the inspecting officer of the location where you store them and make arrangements for the inspection. The inspecting officers may perform an inspection at an office of an authorized agency of the United States if previous arrangements are made. Recruiters or referrers for a fee who designate an employer to complete employment verification procedures may present photocopies or printed electronic images of Forms I-9 at an inspection. If you refuse or delay an inspection, you will be in violation of DHS retention requirements.

At the time of an inspection, you must:

1. Retrieve and reproduce only the Forms I-9 electronically retained in the electronic storage system and supporting documentation specifically requested by the inspecting officer. Supporting documentation includes associated audit trails that show the actions

performed within or on the system during a given period of time.

2. Provide the inspecting officer with appropriate hardware and software, personnel, and documentation necessary to locate, retrieve, read, and reproduce any electronically stored Forms I-9, any supporting documents, and their associated audit trails, reports, and other data used to maintain the authenticity, integrity, and reliability of the records.

3. Provide the inspecting officer, if requested, any reasonably available or obtainable electronic summary file(s), such as spreadsheets, containing all of the information fields on all of the electronically stored Forms I-9.

NOTE: E-Verify employers should provide E-Verify case summaries in addition to Forms I-9 when they receive a request for inspection.

Part Four
Unlawful Discrimination and Penalties
for Prohibited Practices

Unlawful Discrimination
General Provisions

The anti-discrimination provision of the Immigration and Nationality Act (INA), as amended, prohibits four types of unlawful conduct:

1. Citizenship or immigration status discrimination;

2. National origin discrimination;

3. Unfair documentary practices during Form I-9 process (document abuse); and

4. Retaliation.

The Office of Special Counsel for Immigration-Related Unfair Employment Practices, Civil Rights Division, Department of Justice (OSC), enforces the anti-discrimination provision of the INA. The U.S. Equal Employment Opportunity Commission (EEOC) enforces Title VII of the Civil Rights Act of 1964 (Title VII), as amended, and other federal laws that prohibit employment discrimination based on race, color, national origin, religion, sex, age, disability and genetic information.

OSC has exclusive jurisdiction over citizenship or immigration status discrimination claims against all employers with four or more employees. Similarly, OSC has exclusive jurisdiction over all document abuse claims against employers with four or more employees. OSC and EEOC share jurisdiction over national origin discrimination charges. Generally, EEOC has jurisdiction over larger employers with 15 or more employees, whereas OSC has jurisdiction over smaller employers with more than three and less than 15 employees. OSC's jurisdiction over national origin discrimination claims is limited to intentional acts of discrimination with respect to hiring, firing, and recruitment or referral for a fee. Title VII covers both intentional and unintentional acts of discrimination in the workplace, including discrimination in hiring, firing, recruitment, promotion, assignment, compensation, and other terms and conditions of employment.

Types of Employment Discrimination Prohibited Under the INA
Document Abuse

Discriminatory documentary practices related to verifying the employment authorization and identity of employees during the Form I-9 process is called document abuse. Document abuse occurs when employers treat individuals differently on the basis of national origin or citizenship status in the Form I-9 process. Document abuse can be broadly categorized into four types of conduct:

1. Improperly requesting that employees produce more documents than are required by Form I-9 to establish the employee's identity and employment authorization;

2. Improperly requesting that employees present a particular document, such as a "green card," to establish identity and/or employment authorization;

3. Improperly rejecting documents that reasonably appear to be genuine and to relate to the employee presenting them; and

4. Improperly treating groups of applicants differently when completing Form I-9, such as requiring certain groups of employees who look or sound "foreign" to present particular documents the employer does not require other employees to present.

These practices may constitute unlawful document abuse and should be avoided when verifying employment authorization. All employment-authorized individuals are protected against this type of discrimination. The INA's provision against document abuse covers employers with four or more employees.

Citizenship Status Discrimination

Citizenship or immigration status discrimination occurs when an employer treats employees differently based on their real or perceived citizenship or immigration status with respect to hiring, firing, recruitment, or referral for a fee. U.S. citizens, recent permanent residents, temporary residents under the IRCA legalization program, asylees, and refugees are protected. The INA's provision against citizenship or immigration status discrimination covers employers with four or more employees.

National Origin Discrimination

National origin discrimination under the INA occurs when an employer treats employees differently based on their national origin with respect to hiring, firing, recruitment, or referral for a fee. An employee's national origin relates to the employee's place of birth, country of origin, ethnicity, ancestry, native language, accent, or the perception that he or she looks or sounds "foreign." All U.S. citizens and employment-authorized individuals are protected from national origin discrimination. The INA's provision against national origin discrimination generally covers employers with more than three and less than 15 employees. EEOC has jurisdiction over national origin claims involving employers with 15 or more employees.

Retaliation

Retaliation occurs when an employer or other covered entity intimidates, threatens, coerces, or otherwise retaliates against an individual because the individual has filed an immigration-related employment discrimination charge or complaint; has testified or participated in any immigration-related employment discrimination investigation, proceeding, or hearing; or otherwise asserts his or her rights under the INA's anti-discrimination provision.

Types of Discrimination Prohibited by Title VII and Other Federal Anti-discrimination Laws

As noted above, Title VII and other federal laws also prohibit employment discrimination on the basis of national origin, as well as race, color, religion, sex, age, disability and genetic information. EEOC has jurisdiction over employers that employ 15 or more employees for 20 or more weeks in the preceding or current calendar year, and prohibits discrimination in any aspect of employment, including: hiring and firing; compensation, assignment, or classification of employees; transfer, promotion, layoff, or recall; job advertisements; recruitment; testing; use of company facilities; training and apprenticeship programs; fringe benefits; pay, retirement plans, and leave; or other terms and conditions of employment.

Avoiding Discrimination in Recruiting, Hiring, and the Form I-9 Process

In practice, you should treat employees equally when recruiting and hiring, and when verifying employment

authorization and identity during the Form I-9 process. You should not:

1. Set different employment eligibility verification standards or require that different documents be presented by employees because of their national origin and citizenship status. For example, you cannot demand that non-U.S. citizens present DHS-issued documents. Each employee must be allowed to choose the documents that he or she will present from the lists of acceptable Form I-9 documents. For example, both citizens and employment-authorized aliens may present a driver's license (List B) and an unrestricted Social Security card (List C) to establish identity and employment authorization. However, documents that are clearly inconsistent may be rejected.

2. Request to see employment eligibility verification documents before hire and completion of Form I-9 because someone looks or sounds "foreign," or because someone states that he or she is not a U.S. citizen.

3. Refuse to accept a document, or refuse to hire an individual, because a document has a future expiration date.

4. Request that, during reverification, an employee present a new unexpired Employment Authorization Document (Form I-766) if he or she presented one during initial verification. For reverification, each employee must be free to choose to present any document either from List A or from List C.

5. Limit jobs to U.S. citizens unless U.S. citizenship is required for the specific position by law; regulation; executive order; or federal, state, or local government contract. On an individual basis, you may legally prefer a U.S. citizen or noncitizen national over an equally qualified alien to fill a specific position, but you may not adopt a blanket policy of always preferring citizens over noncitizens.

Procedures for Filing Charges of Employment Discrimination

OSC

Discrimination charges may be filed by an individual who believes he or she is the victim of employment discrimination, a person acting on behalf of such an individual, or a DHS officer who has reason to believe that discrimination has occurred.

Discrimination charges must be filed with OSC within 180 days of the alleged discriminatory act. Upon receipt of a complete discrimination charge, OSC will notify you within 10 days that a charge has been filed against you and commence its investigation. If OSC has not filed a complaint with an administrative law judge within 120 days of receiving a charge of discrimination, it will notify the charging party (other than a DHS officer) of his or her right to file a complaint with an administrative law judge within 90 days after receiving the notice. Additionally, OSC may still file a complaint within this 90-day period. If a complaint is filed, the administrative law judge will conduct a hearing and issue a decision. OSC may also attempt to settle a charge, or the parties may enter into a settlement agreement resolving the charge.

EEOC

A charge must be filed with EEOC within 180 days from the date of the alleged violation to protect the charging party's rights. This 180-day filing deadline is extended to 300 days if the charge also is covered by a state or local anti-discrimination law.

Employers Prohibited From Retaliating Against Employees

You cannot take retaliatory action against a person who has filed a charge of discrimination with OSC or EEOC, was a witness or otherwise participated in the investigation or prosecution of a discrimination complaint, or otherwise asserts his or her rights under the INA's anti-discrimination provision and/or Title VII. Such retaliatory action may constitute a violation of the INA's anti-discrimination provision, Title VII, and other federal anti-discrimination law. Retaliation violates federal law.

Additional Information

For more information relating to discrimination based upon national origin and citizenship or immigration status, and discrimination during the Form I-9 process, contact OSC at 1-800-255-8155 (employer hotline) or 1-800-237-2515 (TDD for hearing impaired); or visit OSC's website at www.justice.gov/crt/osc.

For more information on Title VII and EEOC policies and procedures, call 1-800-669-4000, or 1-800-669-6820 (TDD for hearing impaired), or visit EEOC's website at www.eeoc.gov.

Penalties for Prohibited Practices

Unlawful Employment

Civil Penalties

DHS or an administrative law judge may impose penalties if an investigation reveals that you knowingly hired or knowingly continued to employ an unauthorized alien, or failed to comply with the employment eligibility verification requirements with respect to employees hired after November 6, 1986.

DHS will issue a Notice of Intent to Fine (NIF) when it intends to impose penalties. If you receive an NIF, you may request a hearing before an administrative law judge. If your request for a hearing is not received within 30 days, DHS will impose the penalty and issue a Final Order, which cannot be appealed.

Hiring or continuing to employ unauthorized aliens

If DHS or an administrative law judge determines that you have knowingly hired unauthorized aliens (or are continuing to employ aliens knowing that they are or have become unauthorized to work in the United States), you may be ordered to cease and desist from such activity and pay a civil money penalty as follows:

1. First Offense: Not less than $375 and not more than $3,200 for each unauthorized alien

2. Second offense: Not less than $3,200 and not more than $6,500 for each unauthorized alien

3. Subsequent Offenses: Not less than $4,300 and not more than $16,000 for each unauthorized alien.

You will be considered to have knowingly hired an unauthorized alien if, after November 6, 1986, you use a contract, subcontract or exchange, entered into, renegotiated or extended, to obtain the labor of an alien and know the alien is not authorized to work in the United States. You will be subject to the penalties set forth above.

Failing to comply with Form I-9 requirements

If you fail to properly complete, retain, and/or make available for inspection Forms I-9 as required by law, you may face civil money penalties in an amount of not less than $110 and not more than $1,100 for each violation. In determining the amount of the penalty, DHS considers:

1. The size of the business of the employer being charged,

2. The good faith of the employer,

3. The seriousness of the violation,

4. Whether or not the individual was an unauthorized alien, and

5. The history of previous violations of the employer.

Enjoining pattern or practice violations

If the Attorney General has reasonable cause to believe that a person or entity is engaged in a pattern or practice of employment, recruitment or referral in violation of section 274A(a)(1)(A) or (2) of the INA (found at 8 U.S.C. 1324a(a)(1)(A) or (2)), the Attorney General may bring civil action in the appropriate U.S. District Court requesting relief, including a permanent or temporary injunction, restraining order, or other order against the person or entity, as the Attorney General deems necessary.

Requiring indemnification

Employers found to have required a bond or indemnity from an employee against liability under the employer sanctions laws may be ordered to pay a civil money penalty of $1,100 for each violation and to make restitution, either to the person who was required to pay the indemnity, or, if that person cannot be located, to the U.S. Treasury.

Good faith defense

If you can show that you have, in good faith, complied with Form I-9 requirements, then you may have established a "good faith" defense with respect to a charge of knowingly hiring an unauthorized alien, unless the government can show that you had actual knowledge of the unauthorized status of the employee.

A good faith attempt to comply with the paperwork requirements of section 274A(b) of the INA may be adequate notwithstanding a technical or procedural failure to comply, unless you fail to correct a violation within 10 days after notice from DHS.

Criminal Penalties

Engaging in a pattern or practice of knowingly hiring or continuing to employ unauthorized aliens

Persons or entities who are convicted of having engaged in a pattern or practice of knowingly hiring unauthorized aliens (or continuing to employ aliens knowing that they are or have become unauthorized to work in the United States) after November 6, 1986, may face fines of up to $3,000 per employee and/or six months imprisonment.

Engaging in fraud or false statements, or otherwise misusing visas, immigration permits, and identity documents

Persons who use fraudulent identification or employment authorization documents or documents that were lawfully issued to another person, or who make a false statement or attestation to satisfy the employment eligibility verification requirements, may be fined, or imprisoned for up to five years, or both. Other federal criminal statutes may provide higher penalties in certain fraud cases.

Unlawful Discrimination

If an investigation reveals that you engaged in unfair immigration-related employment practices under the INA, OSC may take action. You will be ordered to stop the prohibited practice and may be ordered to take one or more corrective steps, including:

1. Hiring or reinstating, with or without back pay, individuals directly injured by the discrimination;

2. Posting notices to employees about their rights and about employers' obligations; and/or

3. Educating all personnel involved in hiring about complying with the employer sanctions and anti-discrimination laws about the requirements of these laws.

The court may award attorneys' fees to prevailing parties, other than the United States, if it determines that the losing parties' argument is without foundation in law and fact.

Employers who commit citizenship status or national origin discrimination in violation of the anti-discrimination provision of the INA may also be ordered to pay a civil money penalty as follows:

1. First Offense: Not less than $375 and not more than $3,200 for each individual discriminated against.

2. Second Offense: Not less than $3,200 and not more than $6,500 for each individual discriminated against.

3. Subsequent Offenses: Not less than $4,300 and not more than $16,000 for each individual discriminated against.

Employers who commit document abuse in violation of the anti-discrimination provision of the INA may similarly be ordered to pay a civil money penalty of not less than $110 and not more than $1,100 for each individual discriminated against.

If you are found to have committed national origin or other prohibited discrimination under Title VII or other federal law, you may be ordered to stop the prohibited practice and to take one or more corrective steps, including:

1. Hiring, reinstating or promoting with back pay, benefits, and retroactive seniority;

2. Posting notices to employees about their rights and about the employer's obligations; and/or

3. Removing incorrect information, such as a false warning, from an employee's personnel file.

Under Title VII, compensatory damages may also be available where intentional discrimination is found. Damages may be available to compensate for actual monetary losses, for future monetary losses, and for mental anguish and inconvenience. Punitive damages may be available if you acted with malice or reckless indifference.

You may also be required to pay attorneys' fees, expert witness fees, and court costs.

Civil Document Fraud

If a DHS investigation reveals that an individual has knowingly committed or participated in acts relating to document fraud, DHS may take action. DHS will issue an NIF when it intends to impose penalties. Persons who receive an NIF may request a hearing before an administrative law judge. If DHS does not receive a request for a hearing within 30 days, it will impose the penalty and issue a Final Order, which is final and cannot be appealed.

Individuals found by DHS or an administrative law judge to have violated section 274C of the INA may be ordered to cease and desist from such behavior and to pay a civil money penalty as follows:

1. First offense: Not less than $375 and not more than $3,200 for each fraudulent document that is the subject of the violation.

2. Subsequent offenses: Not less than $3,200 and not more than $6,500 for each fraudulent document that is the subject of the violation.

Page intentionally left blank

Part Five
Instructions for Recruiters and Referrers for a Fee

Under the Immigration and Nationality Act (INA), it is unlawful for an agricultural association, agricultural employer, or farm labor contractor to hire, recruit, or refer for a fee an individual for employment in the United States without complying with employment eligibility verification requirements. This provision applies to those agricultural associations, agricultural employers, and farm labor contractors who recruit persons for a fee, and those who refer persons or provide documents or information about persons to employers in return for a fee.

This limited class of recruiters and referrers for a fee must complete Form I-9 when a person they refer is hired. Form I-9 must be fully completed within three business days of the date employment begins, or, in the case of an individual hired for fewer than three business days, at the time employment begins.

Recruiters and referrers for a fee may designate agents, such as national associations or employers, to complete the verification procedures on their behalf. If the employer is designated as the agent, the employer should provide the recruiter or referrer with a photocopy of Form I-9. However, recruiters and referrers for a fee are still responsible for compliance with the law and may be found liable for violations of the law.

Recruiters and referrers for a fee must retain Form I-9 for three years after the date the referred individual was hired by the employer. They must also make Forms I-9 available for inspection by a DHS, DOL, or OSC officer.

NOTE: This does not preclude DHS or DOL from obtaining warrants based on probable cause for entry onto the premises of suspected violators without advance notice.

The penalties for failing to comply with Form I-9 requirements and for requiring indemnification apply to this limited class of recruiters and referrers for a fee.

NOTE: All recruiters and referrers for a fee are still liable for knowingly recruiting or referring for a fee aliens not authorized to work in the United States.

Page intentionally left blank

Part Six
E-Verify: The Web-based Verification Companion to Form I-9

Since verification of the employment authorization and identity of new hires became law in 1986, Form I-9 has been the foundation of the verification process. To improve the accuracy and integrity of this process, USCIS operates an electronic employment verification system called E-Verify.

E-Verify provides an automated link to federal databases to help employers confirm the employment authorization of new hires. E-Verify is free to employers and is available in all 50 states, as well as U.S. territories except for American Samoa.

Employers who participate in E-Verify must complete Form I-9 for each newly hired employee in the United States. E-Verify employers may accept any document or combination of documents on Form I-9, but if the employee chooses to present a List B and C combination, the List B (identity only) document must have a photograph.

After completing a Form I-9 for your new employee, create a case in E-Verify that includes information from Sections 1 and 2 of Form I-9. After creating the case, you will receive a response from E-Verify regarding the employment authorization of the employee. In some cases, E-Verify will provide a response indicating a tentative nonconfirmation of the employee's employment authorization. This does not mean that the employee is necessarily unauthorized to work in the United States. Rather, it means that E-Verify is unable to immediately confirm the employee's authorization to work. In the case of a tentative nonconfirmation, both you and the employee must take steps specified by E-Verify to resolve the status of the case within the prescribed time period.

You must also follow certain procedures when using E-Verify that were designed to protect employees from unfair employment actions. You must use E-Verify for all new hires, both U.S. citizens and noncitizens, and may not use the system selectively. You may not prescreen applicants for employment, check employees hired before the company became a participant in E-Verify (except contractors with a federal contract that requires use of E-Verify), or reverify employees who have temporary employment authorization. You may not terminate or take other adverse action against an employee based on a tentative nonconfirmation.

E-Verify strengthens the Form I-9 employment eligibility verification process that all employers, by law, must follow. By adding E-Verify to the existing Form I-9 employment eligibility verification process, a company can benefit from knowing that it has taken constructive steps toward maintaining a legal workforce.

You can enroll online for E-Verify at www.dhs.gov/E-Verify, which provides instructions for completing the enrollment process. For more information, contact E-Verify at 888-464-4218, or visit the website listed above.

Federal Contractors

On November 14, 2008, the Civilian Agency Acquisition Council and the Defense Acquisition Regulations Council issued a final rule amending the Federal Acquisition Regulation (FAR) (FAR case 2007-013, Employment Eligibility Verification). This regulation was originally scheduled to be effective on January 15, 2009, but the effective date was delayed until September 8, 2009. The regulation requires contractors with a federal contract that contains a FAR E-Verify clause to use E-Verify for their new hires and all employees (existing and new) assigned to the contract. Federal contracts issued on or after September 8, 2009, as well as older contracts that have been modified, may contain the FAR E-Verify clause.

Federal contractors who have a Federal contract that contains the FAR E-Verify clause must follow special rules when completing and updating Forms I-9. For more information, please see the *E-Verify Supplemental Guide for Federal Contractors* available at www.dhs.gov/E-Verify.

Page intentionally left blank

Part Seven
Some Questions You May Have About Form I-9

Employers should read these questions and answers carefully. They contain valuable information that, in some cases, is not found elsewhere in this Handbook.

Questions About the Verification Process

1. **Q.** Do citizens and noncitizen nationals of the United States need to complete Form I-9?

   A. Yes. While citizens and noncitizen nationals of the United States are automatically eligible for employment, they too must present the required documents and complete a Form I-9. U.S. citizens include persons born in the United States, Puerto Rico, Guam, the U.S. Virgin Islands, and the Commonwealth of the Northern Mariana Islands. U.S. noncitizen nationals are persons who owe permanent allegiance to the United States, which include those born in American Samoa, including Swains Island.

   NOTE: Citizens of the Federated States of Micronesia (FSM) and the Republic of the Marshall Islands (RMI) are not noncitizen nationals.

2. **Q.** Do I need to complete Form I-9 for employees working in the CNMI?

   A. Yes. You need to complete Form I-9 for employees hired for employment in the CNMI on or after November 27, 2011. Employers in CNMI should have used Form I-9 CNMI between November 28, 2009 and November 27, 2011. If the employer did not complete Form I-9 CNMI as required during this period the employer should complete a new Form I-9 as soon as the employer discovers the omission. You should not complete Form I-9 for any employees already working for you on November 27, 2009, even if you assign them new job responsibilities within your company. For more information on federal immigration law in the CNMI, go to www.uscis.gov/CNMI.

3. **Q.** If someone accepts a job with my company but will not start work for a month, can I complete Form I-9 when the employee accepts the job?

   A. Yes. The law requires that you complete Form I-9 only when the person actually begins working for pay. However, you may complete the form earlier, as long as the person has been offered and has accepted the job. You may not use the Form I-9 process to screen job applicants.

4. **Q.** Do I need to fill out Forms I-9 for independent contractors or their employees?

   A. No. For example, if you contract with a construction company to perform renovations on your building, you do not have to complete Forms I-9 for that company's employees. The construction company is responsible for completing Forms I-9 for its own employees. However, you may not use a contract, subcontract or exchange to obtain the labor or services of an employee knowing that the employee is unauthorized to work.

5. **Q.** May I fire an employee who fails to produce the required documents within three business days of his or her start date?

   A. Yes. You may terminate an employee who fails to produce the required document or documents, or an acceptable receipt for a document, within three business days of the date employment begins.

6. **Q.** What happens if I properly complete and retain a Form I-9 and DHS discovers that my employee is not actually authorized to work?

   A. You cannot be charged with a verification violation. You will also have a good faith defense against the imposition of employer sanctions penalties for knowingly hiring an unauthorized individual, unless the government can show you had knowledge of the unauthorized status of the employee.

Questions about Documents

7. **Q.** **May I specify which documents I will accept for verification?**

    A. No. The employee may choose which document(s) he or she wants to present from the Lists of Acceptable Documents. You must accept any document (from List A) or combination of documents (one from List B and one from List C) listed on Form I-9 and found in Part Eight of this Handbook that reasonably appear on their face to be genuine and to relate to the person presenting them. To do otherwise could be an unfair immigration-related employment practice in violation of the anti-discrimination provision in the INA. Individuals who look and/ or sound foreign must not be treated differently in the recruiting, hiring, or verification process. For more information relating to discrimination during the Form I-9 process, contact OSC at 1-800-255-8155 (employers) or 1-800-237-2515 (TDD) or visit OSC's website at www.justice.gov/crt/osc.

    NOTE: An employer participating in E-Verify can only accept a List B document with a photograph.

8. **Q.** **If an employee enters an Alien Number or Admission Number when completing Section 1 of Form I-9, may I ask to see a document with that number?**

    A. No. Although it is your responsibility as an employer to ensure that your employees fully complete Section 1 at the time employment begins, the employee is not required to present a document to complete this section.

    When you complete Section 2, you may not ask to see a document with the employee's Alien Number or Admission Number or otherwise specify which document(s) an employee may present.

9. **Q.** **What is my responsibility concerning the authenticity of document(s) presented to me?**

    A. You must examine the document(s), and if they reasonably appear on their face to be genuine and to relate to the person presenting them, you must accept them. To do otherwise could be an

unfair immigration-related employment practice. If the document(s) do not reasonably appear on their face to be genuine or to relate to the person presenting them, you must not accept them.

10. **Q.** **My employee has presented a U.S. passport card. Is this an acceptable document?**

    A. Yes. The passport card is a wallet-size document issued by the U.S. Department of State. While its permissible uses for international travel are more limited than the U.S. passport book, the passport card is a fully valid passport that attests to the U.S. citizenship and identity of the bearer. As such, the passport card is considered a "passport" for purposes of Form I-9 and has been included on List A of the Lists of Acceptable Documents on Form I-9.

11. **Q.** **Why was documentation for citizens of the Federated States of Micronesia (FSM) and the Republic of the Marshall Islands (RMI) added to the Lists of Acceptable Documents on Form I-9?**

    A. Under the Compacts of Free Association between the United States and FSM and RMI, most citizens of FSM and RMI are eligible to reside and work in the United States as nonimmigrants. An amendment to the Compacts eliminated the need for citizens of these two countries to obtain Employment Authorization Documents (Forms I-766) to work in the United States. However, FSM and RMI citizens may also apply for Employment Authorization Documents (Forms I-766) if they wish, or present a combination of List B and List C documents. The List A document specific to FSM and RMI citizens is a valid FSM or RMI passport with a Form I-94/Form I-94A indicating nonimmigrant admission under one of the Compacts.

12. **Q.** **How do I know whether a Native American tribal document issued by a U.S. tribe presented by my employee is acceptable for Form I-9 purposes?**

    A. In order to be acceptable, a Native American tribal document should be issued by a tribe recognized by the U.S. federal government. Because federal recognition of tribes can change over time, to determine if the tribe is federally recognized, please check the Bureau of Indian Affairs website at www.bia.gov.

13. Q. **The Native American tribal document is listed on both List B and List C of Form I-9. Does this mean that my employee may present this document to prove both identity and employment authorization?**

A. If an employee presents a Native American tribal document, it establishes both identity and employment authorization on Form I-9, so you do not need any other documents from the employee to complete Section 2 of Form I-9.

14. Q. **Can the Certificate of Indian Status, commonly referred to as the status card or INAC card, be used as a Native American tribal document for Form I-9 purposes?**

A. No. This card is not a Native American tribal document. It is issued by Indian and Northern Affairs Canada (INAC), which is a part of the Canadian government.

15. Q. **An employee has attested to being a U.S. citizen or U.S. noncitizen national on Section 1 of Form I-9, but has presented me with Form I-551, Permanent Resident Card, or "green card." Another employee has attested to being a lawful permanent resident but has presented a U.S. passport. Should I accept these documents?**

A. In these situations, you should first ensure that the employee understood and properly completed the Section 1 attestation of status. If the employee made a mistake and corrects the attestation, he or she should initial and date the correction, or complete a new Form I-9. If the employee confirms the accuracy of his or her initial attestation, you should not accept a "green card" from a U.S. citizen or a U.S. passport from an alien. Although you are not expected to be an immigration law expert, both documents in question are inconsistent with the status attested to and are, therefore, not documents that reasonably relate to the person presenting them.

16. Q. **May I accept an expired document?**

A. No. Expired documents are no longer acceptable for Form I-9. However, you may accept Employment Authorization Documents (Forms I-766) and Permanent Resident Cards (Forms I-551) that appear to be expired on their face, but have been extended by USCIS.

For example, Temporary Protected Status (TPS) beneficiaries whose Employment Authorization Documents (Forms I-766) appear to be expired may be automatically extended in a Federal Register notice. These individuals may continue to work based on their expired Employment Authorization Documents (Forms I-766) during the automatic extension period specified in the Federal Register notice. When the automatic extension of the Employment Authorization Document (Form I-766) expires, you must reverify the employee's employment authorization.

Please see Part 2 for more information on TPS.

NOTE: Some documents, such as birth certificates and Social Security cards, do not contain an expiration date and should be treated as unexpired.

17. Q. **How can I tell if a DHS-issued document has expired? If it has expired, should I reverify the employee?**

A. Some INS-issued documents, such as older versions of the Alien Registration Receipt Card (Form I-551), do not have expiration dates, and are still acceptable for Form I-9 purposes. However, all subsequent DHS-issued Permanent Resident Cards (Forms I-551) contain two-year or 10-year expiration dates. You should not reverify an expired Alien Registration Receipt Card/Permanent Resident Card (Form I-551). Other DHS-issued documents, such as the Employment Authorization Document (Form I-766) also have expiration dates. These dates can be found on the face of the document. Generally, Employment Authorization Documents (Forms I-766) must be reverified upon expiration.

18. Q. **Some employees have presented Social Security Administration printouts with their name, Social Security number, date of birth, and their parents' names as proof of employment authorization. May I accept such printouts in place of a Social Security card as evidence of employment authorization?**

A. No. Only a person's official Social Security card or a receipt for a replacement card issued by SSA is acceptable.

19. **Q.** What should I do if an employee presents a Social Security card marked "NOT VALID FOR EMPLOYMENT," but states that he or she is now authorized to work?

A. You should ask the employee to provide another document to establish his or her employment authorization, since such Social Security cards do not establish this and are not acceptable documents for Form I-9. Such an employee should go to the local SSA office with proof of his or her lawful employment status to be issued a Social Security card without employment restrictions.

20. **Q.** May I accept a photocopy of a document presented by an employee?

A. No. Employees must present original documents. The only exception is that an employee may present a certified copy of a birth certificate.

21. **Q.** I noticed on Form I-9 that under List A there are three spaces for document numbers and expiration dates. Does this mean I have to see three List A documents.

A. No. Form I-9 (Rev. 03/08/13N) includes an expanded document entry area in Section 2. The additional spaces are provided in case an employee presents a List A document that is really a combination of more than one document. For example, an F-1 student in curricular practical training may present, under List A, a foreign passport, Form I-94/Form I-94A and Form I-20 that specifies that you are his or her approved employer. Form I-9 provides space for you to enter the document number and expiration date for all three documents. Another instance where an employer may need to enter document information for three documents is for J-1 exchange visitors. If an employee provides you with one document from List A (e.g., U.S. passport), or a combination of 2 documents (e.g., foreign passport and Form I-94/94A), you do not need to fill out any unused space(s) under List A.

22. **Q.** When I review an employee's identity and employment authorization documents, should I make copies of them?

A. If you participate in E-Verify and the employee presents a document used as part of Photo Matching, currently the U.S. passport and passport card, Permanent Resident Card (Form I-551) and the Employment Authorization Document (Form I-766), you must retain a photocopy of the document he or she presents. Other documents may be added to Photo Matching in the future. If you do not participate in E-Verify, you are not required to make photocopies of documents. However, if you wish to make photocopies of documents other than those used in E-Verify, you must do so for all employees. Photocopies must not be used for any other purpose. Photocopying documents does not relieve you of your obligation to fully complete Section 2 of Form I-9, nor is it an acceptable substitute for proper completion of Form I-9 in general.

23. **Q.** When can employees present receipts for documents in lieu of actual documents from the Lists of Acceptable Documents?

A. The "receipt rule" is designed to cover situations in which an employee is authorized to work at the time of initial hire or reverification, but he or she is not in possession of a document listed on the Lists of Acceptable Documents accompanying Form I-9. Receipts showing that a person has applied for an initial grant of employment authorization or for renewal of employment authorization are not acceptable.

An individual may present a receipt in lieu of a document listed on Form I-9 to complete Section 2 or Section 3 of Form I-9. The receipt is valid for a temporary period. There are three different documents that qualify as receipts under the rule:

1. A receipt for a replacement document when the document has been lost, stolen, or damaged. The receipt is valid for 90 days, after which the individual must present the replacement document to complete Form I-9.

NOTE: This rule does not apply to individuals who present receipts for new documents following the expiration of their previously held document.

The individual must present Form I-551 by the expiration date of the temporary I-551 stamp or within one year from the date of issuance of Form I-94/Form I-94A if the I-551 stamp does not contain an expiration date.

3. A Form I-94/Form I-94A containing an unexpired refugee admission stamp. This is considered a receipt for either an Employment Authorization Document (Form I-766) or a combination of an unrestricted Social Security card and List B document. The employee must present an Employment Authorization Document (Form I-766) or an unrestricted Social Security card in combination with a List B document to complete Form I-9 within 90 days after the date of hire or, in the case of reverification, the date employment authorization expires. For more information on receipts, see Table 1 in Part 2.

24. Q. **My employee has applied for a new Employment Authorization Document (Form I-766). Is the USCIS receipt notice covered by the Form I-9 receipt rule?**

A. In this case, the USCIS receipt notice is not an acceptable receipt for Form I-9 purposes. An employee with temporary employment authorization and holding an Employment Authorization Document (Form I-766) should apply for a new card at least 90 days before the expiration of his or her current document. If your employee applied for a new card at least 90 days before his or her current card expired but is nearing the end of the 90-day processing period without a decision from USCIS, instruct your employee to call the National Customer Service Center at 1-800-375-5283 or 1-800-767-1833 (TDD) about the status of his or her application. USCIS strongly encourages that employees first call the National Customer Service Center before visiting a USCIS office to prevent possible delays. If your employee prefers to check on the status of his or her application at a USCIS office, he or she may schedule an InfoPass appointment at www.infopass.uscis.gov. When your employee's current Employment Authorization Document (Form I-766) expires, he or she must be able to present a List A document, a List C document, or an acceptable receipt under the receipt rule to satisfy Form I-9 reverification requirements.

25. Q. **My nonimmigrant employee has presented a foreign passport with a Form I-94/Form**

I-94A (List A, Item 5). **How do I know if this employee is authorized to work?**

A. You, as the employer, likely have submitted a petition to USCIS on the nonimmigrant employee's behalf. However, there are some exceptions to this rule:

1. You made an offer of employment to a Canadian passport holder who entered the United States under the North American Free Trade Agreement (NAFTA) with an offer letter from your company. This nonimmigrant worker will have a Form I-94/Form I-94A indicating a TN immigration status, and may choose to present it with his or her passport under List A. The employee may also present Form I-94/Form I-94A indicating a TN immigration status as a List C document, in which case your employee will need to present a List B document (e.g., Canadian driver's license) to satisfy Section 2 of Form I-9.

2. A student working in on-campus employment or participating in curricular practical training. (See Part 2.)

3. A J-1 exchange visitor. (See Part 2.)

Most employees who present a foreign passport in combination with a Form I-94 or I-94A (List A, Item 5) are restricted to work only for the employer who petitioned on their behalf. If you did not submit a petition for an employee who presents such documentation, then that nonimmigrant worker is not usually authorized to work for you. See Part 2 for more information on nonimmigrant employees.

26. Q. **My new employee presented two documents to complete Form I-9, each containing a different last name. One document matches the name she entered in Section 1. The employee explained that she had just gotten married and changed her last name, but had not yet changed the name on the other document. Can I accept the document with the different name?**

A. You may accept a document with a different name than the name entered in Section 1 provided that you resolve the question of whether the document reasonably relates to the employee. You also may wish to attach a brief memo to Form I-9 stating the reason for the name discrepancy, along with any supporting documentation the employee provides. An employee may provide documentation to support his or her name change, but is not required to do so. If, however, you determine that the document with a different name does not reasonably appear to be genuine and to relate to her, you may ask her to provide other documents from the Lists of Acceptable Documents on Form I-9.

27. Q. **My employee entered a compound last name in Section 1 of Form I-9. The documents she presented contain only one of these names. Can I accept this document?**

A. DHS does not require employees to use any specific naming standard for Form I-9. If a new employee enters more than one last name in Section 1, but presents a document that contains only one of those last names, the document he or she presents for Section 2 is acceptable as long as you are satisfied that the document reasonably appears to be genuine and to relate to him or her. It is helpful for individuals attesting to lawful permanent resident status who have more than one name to enter their name on Form I-9 as it appears on their Permanent Resident Card (Form I-551).

28. Q. **The name on the document my employee presented to me is spelled slightly differently than the name she entered in Section 1 of Form I-9. Can I accept this document?**

A. If the document contains a slight spelling variation, and the employee has a reasonable explanation for the variation, the document is acceptable as long as you are satisfied that the document otherwise reasonably appears to be genuine and to relate to him or her.

29. Q. **My employee's Employment Authorization Document (Form I-766) expired and the employee now wants to show me a Social Security card. Do I need to see a current DHS document?**

A. No. During reverification, an employee must be allowed to choose what documentation to present from either List A or List C. If an employee presents an unrestricted Social Security card upon reverification, the employee does not also need to present a current DHS document. However, if an employee presents a restricted Social Security card upon reverification, you must reject the restricted Social Security card, since it is not an acceptable Form I-9 document, and ask the employee to choose different documentation from List A or List C of Form I-9.

30. Q. **Can DHS double-check the status of an individual I hired, or "run" his or her number (typically an Alien Number or Social Security number) and tell me if it is valid?**

A. DHS cannot double-check a number for you, unless you participate in E-Verify, which confirms the employment authorization of your newly hired employees. For more information about this program, see Part Six. You may also call DHS at 1-888-464-4218 or visit www.dhs.gov/E-Verify. You also may contact DHS if you have a strong reason to believe documentation may not be valid, in which case ICE may investigate the possible violation of law.

31. Q. **My employee presented me with a document issued by INS rather than DHS. Can I accept it?**

A. Yes, you can accept a document issued by INS if the document is unexpired and reasonably appears to be genuine and to relate to the individual presenting it. Effective March 1, 2003, the functions of the former INS were transferred to three agencies within the new DHS: USCIS, CBP, and ICE. Most immigration documents acceptable for Form I-9 use are issued by USCIS. Some documents issued by the former INS before March 1, 2003, such as Permanent Resident Cards or Forms I-94 noting asylee status, may still be within their period of validity. If otherwise acceptable, a document should not be rejected because it was issued by INS rather than DHS. It should also be noted that INS documents may bear dates of issuance after March 1, 2003, as it took some time in 2003 to modify document forms to reflect the new USCIS identity.

Questions about Completing and Retaining Form I-9

32. Q. **Can an employee leave any part of Section 1 on Form I-9 blank?**

A. Employees must complete every applicable field in Section 1 of Form I-9 with the exception of the fields requesting the employee's e-mail address, telephone number and Social Security number. However, employees must enter their Social Security number in this field if you participate in E-Verify.

NOTE: Not all employees who attest to being an Alien Authorized to Work will have an expiration date for their employment authorization. However, refugees and asylees who present an Employment Authorization Document (Form I-766) have employment authorization that does not expire. These individuals should put "N/A" where Section 1 asks for an expiration date.

33. Q. **How do I correct a mistake on an employee's Form I-9?**

A. The best way to correct Form I-9 is to line through the portions of the form that contain incorrect information, then enter the correct information. Initial and date your correction. If you have previously made changes on Forms I-9 in White-Out instead, USCIS recommends that you attach a note to the corrected Forms I-9 explaining what happened. Be sure to sign and date the note.

34. Q. **What should I do if I need to reverify an employee who filled out an earlier version of Form I-9?**

A. If you used a version of Form I-9 when you originally verified the employee that is no longer valid, and you are now reverifying the employment authorization of that employee, the employee must provide any document(s) he or she chooses from the current Lists of Acceptable Documents. Enter this new document(s) in Section 3 of the current version of Form I-9 and retain it with the previously completed Form I-9. To see if your form is an acceptable version of Form I-9, go to www.uscis.gov/I-9.

For more information on reverification, please see Part 2.

35. Q. **Do I need to complete a new Form I-9 when one of my employees is promoted within my company or transfers to another company office at a different location?**

A. No. You do not need to complete a new Form I-9 for employees who have been promoted or transferred.

36. Q. **What do I do when an employee's employment authorization expires?**

A. To continue to employ an individual whose employment authorization has expired, you will need to reverify him or her in Section 3 of Form I-9. Reverification must occur no later than the date that employment authorization expires. The employee must present a document from either List A or List C that shows either an extension of his or her initial employment authorization or new employment authorization. You must review this document and, if it reasonably appears on its face to be genuine and to relate to the person presenting it, enter the document title, number, and expiration date (if any), in the Updating and Reverification Section (Section 3), and sign in the appropriate space.

If the version of Form I-9 that you used for the employee's original verification is no longer valid, you must complete Section 3 of the current Form I-9 upon reverification and attach it to the original Form I-9.

You may want to establish a calendar call-up system for employees whose employment authorization will expire and provide the employee with at least 90 days notice prior to the expiration date of the employment authorization.

You may not reverify an expired U.S. passport or passport card, an Alien Registration Receipt Card/Permanent Resident Card (Form I-551), or a List B document that has expired.

NOTE: You cannot refuse to accept a document because it has a future expiration date. You must accept any document (from List A or List C) listed on Form I-9 that on its face reasonably appears to be genuine and to relate to the person presenting it. To do otherwise could be an unfair immigration-related employment practice in violation of the anti-discrimination provision of the INA.

37. Q. Can I avoid reverifying an employee on Form I-9 by not hiring persons whose employment authorization has an expiration date?

A. No. You cannot refuse to hire persons solely because their employment authorization is temporary. The existence of a future expiration date does not preclude continuous employment authorization for an employee and does not mean that subsequent employment authorization will not be granted. In addition, consideration of a future employment authorization expiration date in determining whether an individual is qualified for a particular job may be an unfair immigration-related employment practice in violation of the anti-discrimination provision of the INA.

38. Q. As an employer, do I have to fill out all the Forms I-9 myself?

A. No. You may designate someone to fill out Forms I-9 for you, such as a personnel officer, foreman, agent, or anyone else acting on your behalf, such as a notary public. Please note that if someone else fills out Form I-9 on your behalf, he or she must carry out full Form I-9 responsibilities. However, you are still liable for any violations in connection with the form or the verification process.

For example, it is not acceptable for a notary public to view employment authorization and identity documents, but leave Section 2 for you to complete. The person who views an employee's employment authorization documents should also complete and sign Section 2 on your behalf.

39. Q. Can I contract with someone to complete Forms I-9 for my business?

A. Yes. You can contract with another person or business to verify employees' identities and employment authorization and to complete Forms I-9 for you. However, you are still responsible for the contractor's actions and are liable for any violations of the employer sanctions laws.

40. Q. I use a professional employer organization (PEO) that co-employs my employees. Am I responsible for Form I-9 compliance for these employees or is the PEO?

A. Co-employment arrangements can take many forms. As an employer, you continue to be responsible for compliance with Form I-9 requirements.

If the arrangement into which you have entered is one where an employer-employee relationship also exists between the PEO and the employee (e.g., the employee performs labor or services for the PEO), the PEO would be considered an employer for Form I-9 purposes and:

- The PEO may rely upon the previously completed Form I-9 at the time of initial hire for each employee continuing employment as a co-employee of you and the PEO, or

- The PEO may choose to complete new Forms I-9 at the time of co-employment.

If more co-employees are subsequently hired, only one Form I-9 must be completed by either the PEO or the client. However, both you and your PEO are responsible for complying with Form I-9 requirements, and DHS may impose penalties on either party for failure to do so. Penalties for verification violations, if any, may vary depending on:

1. A party's control or lack of control over the Form I-9 process,

2. Size of the business,

3. Good faith in complying with Form I-9 requirements,

4. The seriousness of the party's violation,

5. Whether or not the employee was authorized to work,

6. The history of the party's previous violations and

7. Other relevant factors.

41. Q. Our company acquired another company, along with its employees. Are we required to complete Forms I-9 for these employees?

A. Employers who have acquired another company or have merged with another company have two options:

- **Option A:** Treat all acquired employees as new hires and complete a new Form I-9 for each and every individual irrespective of when that employee was originally hired. Enter the effective date of acquisition or merger as the date the employee began employment in Section 2 of the new Form I-9.

- **Option B:** Treat acquired individuals as employees who are continuing in their uninterrupted employment status and retain the previous owner's Forms I-9 for each acquired employee. Note that you are liable for any errors or omissions on the previously completed Forms I-9.

NOTE: Employees hired on or before November 6, 1986, who are continuing in their employment and have a reasonable expectation of employment at all times, are exempt from completing Form I-9 and cannot be verified in E-Verify. For making this determination, see 8 CFR 274a.2(b)(1)(B)(viii) and 8 CFR 274a.7. If you determine that an employee hired on or before November 6, 1986 is not continuing in his or her employment or does not have a reasonable expectation of employment at all times, the employee may be required to complete a Form I-9.

If you choose to complete new Forms I-9 (Option A), in order to ensure that you do not engage in discrimination, you must do so for all of your acquired employees, without regard to actual or perceived citizenship status or national origin.

Federal contractors with the FAR E-Verify clause have special rules relating to the verification of existing employees. For more information, see the *E-Verify Supplemental Guide for Federal Contractors* at www.uscis.gov/E-Verify.

Mergers and acquisitions can be a very complicated area of the law and determining whether or not employees are continuing in their employment with the new entity for Form I-9 purposes is often not clear. For that reason USCIS strongly recommends that any business con-

fronted with this issue should consider retaining private legal counsel.

42. **Q. How does OSC obtain the necessary information to determine whether an employer has committed an unfair immigration-related employment practice under the anti-discrimination provision of the INA?**

A. OSC will notify you in writing to initiate an investigation, request information and documents, and interview your employees. If you refuse to cooperate, OSC can obtain a subpoena to compel you to produce the information requested or to appear for an investigative interview.

43. **Q. Do I have to complete Forms I-9 for Canadians or Mexicans who entered the United States under the North American Free Trade Agreement (NAFTA)?**

A. Yes. You must complete Forms I-9 for all employees. NAFTA entrants must show identity and employment authorization documents just like all other employees.

44. **Q. If I am a recruiter or referrer for a fee, do I have to fill out Forms I-9 on individuals that I recruit or refer?**

A. No, with three exceptions: Agricultural associations, agricultural employers, and farm labor contractors must complete Forms I-9 on all individuals who are recruited or referred for a fee. However, all recruiters and referrers for a fee must complete Forms I-9 for their own employees hired after November 6, 1986. Also, all recruiters and referrers for a fee are liable for knowingly recruiting or referring for a fee individuals not authorized to work in the United States and must comply with federal anti-discrimination laws.

45. **Q. Can I complete Section 1 of Form I-9 for an employee?**

A. You may help an employee who needs assistance in completing Section 1 of Form I-9. However, you must also complete the Preparer and/or Translator Certification block. The employee must still sign the certification block in Section 1.

46. Q. If I am self-employed, do I have to fill out a Form I-9 on myself?

A. A self-employed person does not need to complete a Form I-9 on his or her own behalf unless the person is an employee of a separate business entity, such as a corporation or partnership. If the person is an employee of a separate business entity, he or she, and any other employees, will have to complete Form I-9.

47. Q. I have heard that some state employment agencies, commonly known as state workforce agencies, can certify that people they refer are authorized to work. Is that true?

A. Yes. A state employment agency may choose to verify the employment authorization and identity of an individual it refers for employment on Form I-9. In such a case, the agency must issue a certification to you so that you receive it within 21 business days from the date the referred individual is hired. If an agency refers a potential employee to you with a job order, other appropriate referral form, or telephonically authorized referral, and the agency sends you a certification within 21 business days of the referral, you do not have to check documents or complete a Form I-9 if you hire that person. Before receiving the certification, you must retain the job order, referral form, or annotation reflecting the telephonically authorized referral as you would Forms I-9. When you receive the certification, you must review the certification to ensure that it relates to the person hired and observe the person sign the certification. You must also retain the certification as you would a Form I-9 and make it available for inspection, if requested. You should check with your state employment agency to see if it provides this service and become familiar with its certification document.

48. Q. How can I protect private information on Forms I-9?

A. Since Form I-9 contains an employee's private information, and you are required to retain forms for specific periods of time, you should ensure that you protect that private information, and that it is used only for Form I-9 purposes. To protect employees' private information, ensure that completed Forms I-9 and all supporting documents, including photocopies of documents, as well as information regarding employment authorization if you participate in E-Verify, are stored in a safe, secure location that only authorized individuals can access. For more information on protecting electronically stored Forms I-9, see Part 3.

Questions about Avoiding Discrimination

49. Q. Can I be charged with discrimination if I contact DHS about a document presented to me that does not reasonably appear to be genuine and to relate to the person presenting it?

A. No. If you are presented with documentation that does not reasonably appear to be genuine or to relate to the employee, you cannot accept that documentation. While you are not legally required to inform DHS of such situations, you may do so if you choose. However, DHS is unable to provide employment eligibility verification services other than through its E-Verify program. If you treat all employees equally and do not single out employees based on their national origin or citizenship status for closer scrutiny, you are unlikely to be found to have engaged in unlawful discrimination.

50. Q. I recently hired someone who checked the fourth box in the immigration status attestation section on Section 1 of Form I-9, indicating that he is an alien. However, his Form I-94 does not contain an expiration date, which appears to be required by the form. What should I do?

A. Refugees and asylees, as well as some other classes of nonimmigrants such as certain citizens of the Federated States of Micronesia and the Republic of the Marshall Islands, are authorized to work because of their status. These nonimmigrants may present a Form I-94/Form I-94A that does not have an expiration date or any combination of documents from the List of Acceptable Documents. Such individuals should check "An alien authorized to work," enter the Alien Number or Admission Number in the first space, and "N/A" in the second space, because their employment authorization does not expire. Refusing to hire employment-authorized individuals because they are unable to provide an expiration date on Form I-9 is a violation of the anti-discrimination provision in the INA.

NOTE: Some foreign students who are authorized to work also may not have a specific expiration date for their employment authorization. See Part 2 for more information.

Questions about Employees Hired On or Before November 6, 1986

51. Q. **Will I be subject to employer sanctions penalties if an employee I hired on or before November 6, 1986 is in the United States illegally?**

A. No. You will not be subject to employer sanctions penalties for retaining an employee who is not authorized to work in the United States if the employee was hired on or before November 6, 1986. However, the fact that the employee was on your payroll on or before November 6, 1986, does not give him or her the right to remain in the United States. Unless the employee obtains permission from DHS to remain in the United States, he or she is subject to apprehension and removal from the United States.

Questions about Different Versions of Form I-9

52. Q. **Is Form I-9 available in different languages?**

A. Form I-9 is available in English and Spanish. However, only employers in Puerto Rico may use the Spanish version to meet the verification and retention requirements of the law. Employers in the United States and other U.S. territories may use the Spanish version as a translation guide for Spanish-speaking employees, but the English version must be completed and retained in the employer's records. Employees may also use or ask for a preparer and/or translator to assist them in completing the form.

53. Q. **Are employers in Puerto Rico required to use the Spanish version of Form I-9?**

A. No. Employers in Puerto Rico may use either the Spanish or the English version of Form I-9 to verify new employees.

54. Q. **May I continue to use earlier versions of Form I-9?**

A. No, employers must use the current version of Form I-9. A revision date with an "N" next to it indicates that all previous versions with earlier revision dates, in English or Spanish, are no longer valid. You may also use subsequent versions that have a "Y" next to the revision date. If in doubt, go to www.uscis.gov/i-9 to view or download the most current form.

55. Q. **Where do I get the Spanish version of Form I-9?**

A. You may download the Spanish version of this form from the USCIS website at www.uscis.gov/i-9. For employers without internet access, you may call the USCIS Forms Request Line toll-free at 1-800-870-3676.

Questions about Military IDs

56. Q. **I know that a valid unexpired military ID card is a valid List B identification document. Is a military ID card ever acceptable as List A evidence of both identity and employment authorization?**

A. Yes, but only if the employer is the U.S. military and the Form I-9 is completed in the context of military enlistment. In the case of an individual lawfully enlisted in the U.S. Armed Forces, a valid, unexpired military ID card may be accepted as a List A document by the Armed Forces only. No other employer may accept a military ID card as a List A document.

For more questions and answers on Form I-9 topics, go to www.uscis.gov/I-9 Central and select I-9 Central Questions & Answers.

Page intentionally left blank

Part Eight
Acceptable Documents for Verifying Employment Authorization and Identity

The following documents have been designated as acceptable for Form I-9 to establish an employee's employment authorization and identity. The comprehensive Lists of Acceptable Documents can be found on the next pages of this Handbook and on the last page of Form I-9. Samples of many of the acceptable documents appear on the following pages.

To establish both identity and employment authorization, a person must present to his or her employer a document or combination of documents, if applicable, from List A, which shows both identity and employment authorization; or one document from List B, which shows only identity, and one document from List C, which shows only employment authorization.

If a person is unable to present the required document(s) within three business days of the date work for pay begins, he or she must present an acceptable receipt within that time. The person then must present the actual document when the receipt period ends. The person must

have indicated on or before the time employment began, by having checked an appropriate box in Section 1, that he or she is already authorized to be employed in the United States. Receipts showing that a person has applied for an initial grant of employment authorization, or for renewal of employment authorization, are not acceptable. Receipts are also not acceptable if employment is for fewer than three business days.

The following pages show the most recent versions and representative images of some of the various acceptable documents on the list. These images can assist you in your review of the document presented to you. These pages are not, however, comprehensive. In some cases, many variations of a particular document exist and new versions may be published subsequent to the publication date of this Handbook. Keep in mind that USCIS does not expect you to be a document expert. You are expected to accept documents that reasonably appear to be genuine and to relate to the person presenting them. For a list of acceptable receipts for Form I-9, see Table 1 in Part Two.

LIST A: Documents That Establish Both Identity and Employment Authorization
All documents must be unexpired.

1. U.S. Passport or Passport Card

2. Permanent Resident Card or Alien Registration Receipt Card (Form I-551)

3. Foreign passport that contains a temporary I-551 stamp or temporary I-551 printed notation on a machine-readable immigrant visa (MRIV)

4. Employment Authorization Document (Card) that contains a photograph (Form I-766)

5. In the case of a nonimmigrant alien authorized to work for a specific employer incident to status, a foreign passport with Form I-94 or Form I-94A bearing the same name as the passport and containing an endorsement of the alien's nonimmigrant status, as long as the period of endorsement has not yet expired and the proposed employment is not in conflict with any restrictions or limitations identified on the form

6. Passport from the Federated States of Micronesia (FSM) or the Republic of the Marshall Islands (RMI) with Form I-94 or Form I-94A indicating nonimmigrant admission under the Compact of Free Association Between the United States and the FSM or RMI

LIST B: Documents That Establish Identity
All documents must be unexpired.

For individuals 18 years of age or older:

1. Driver's license or ID card issued by a state or outlying possession of the United States, provided it contains a photograph or information such as name, date of birth, gender, height, eye color, and address

2. ID card issued by federal, state, or local government agencies or entities, provided it contains a photograph or information such as name, date of birth, gender, height, eye color, and address

3. School ID card with a photograph

4. Voter's registration card

5. U.S. military card or draft record

6. Military dependent's ID card

7. U.S. Coast Guard Merchant Mariner Card

8. Native American tribal document

9. Driver's license issued by a Canadian government authority

For persons under age 18 who are unable to present a document listed above:

10. School record or report card

11. Clinic, doctor, or hospital record

12. Day-care or nursery school record

LIST C: Documents That Establish Employment Authorization
All documents must be unexpired.

1. A Social Security Account Number card unless the card includes one of the following restrictions:

   (1) NOT VALID FOR EMPLOYMENT

   (2) VALID FOR WORK ONLY WITH INS AUTHORIZATION

   (3) VALID FOR WORK ONLY WITH DHS AUTHORIZATION

   NOTE: A copy (such as a metal or plastic reproduction) is not acceptable.

2. Certification of Birth Abroad issued by the U.S. Department of State (Form FS-545)

3. Certification of Report of Birth issued by the U.S. Department of State (Form DS-1350)

4. Original or certified copy of a birth certificate issued by a state, county, municipal authority, or outlying possession of the United States bearing an official seal

5. Native American tribal document

6. U.S. Citizen Identification Card (Form I-197)

7. Identification Card for Use of Resident Citizen in the United States (Form I-179)

8. Employment authorization document issued by DHS

List A—Documents That Establish Both Identity and Employment Authorization

U.S. Passport

The U.S. Department of State issues the U.S. passport to U.S. citizens and noncitizen nationals. There are a small number of versions still in circulation that may differ from the main versions shown here.

The illustrations in this Handbook do not necessarily reflect the actual size of the documents.

Current U.S. Passport cover and open

Older U.S. Passport cover and open

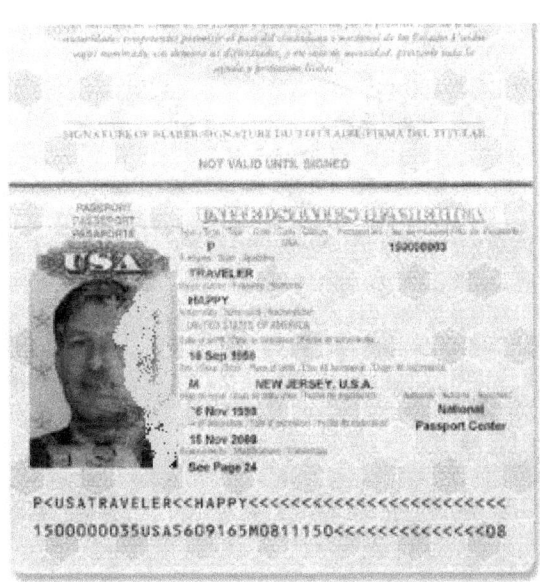

U.S. Passport Card

The U.S. Department of State began producing the passport card in July 2008. The passport card is a wallet-size card that can only be used for land and sea travel between the United States and Canada, Mexico, the Caribbean, and Bermuda.

Passport Card front and back

Permanent Resident Card (Form I-551)

On May 11, 2010, USCIS began issuing the newly re-designed Permanent Resident Card, also known as the Green Card, which is now green in keeping with its long-standing nickname. The card is personalized with the bearer's photo, name, USCIS number, alien registration number, date of birth, and laser-engraved fingerprint, as well as the card expiration date.

Note that on the new card, shown below, the lawful permanent resident's alien registration number, commonly known as the A number, is found under the USCIS # heading. The A number is also located on the back of the card.

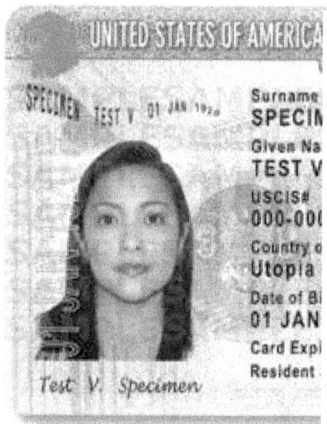 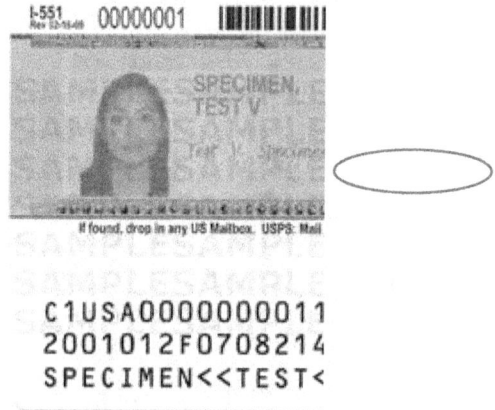

Current Permanent Resident Card (Form I-551) front and back

This most recent older version of the Permanent Resident Card shows the DHS seal and contains a detailed hologram on the front of the card. Each card is personalized with an etching showing the bearer's photo, name, fingerprint, date of birth, alien registration number, card expiration date, and card number.

Also in circulation are older Resident Alien cards, issued by the U.S. Department of Justice, Immigration and Naturalization Service, which do not have expiration dates and are valid indefinitely. These cards are peach in color and contain the bearer's fingerprint and photograph.

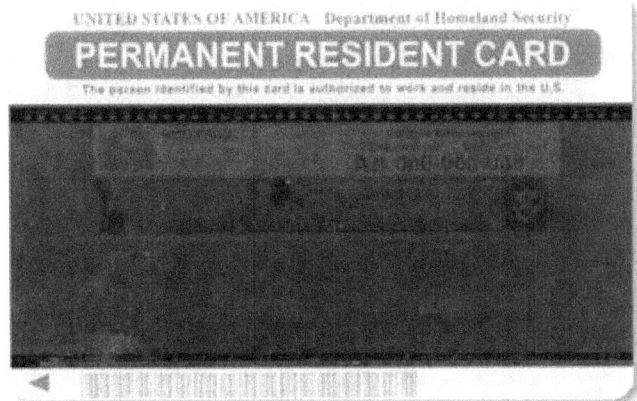

Older version Permanent Resident Card (Form I-551) front and back

Foreign Passport with I-551 Stamp or MRIV

Unexpired Foreign Passport with I-551 Stamp

USCIS uses either an I-551 stamp or a temporary I-551 printed notation on a machine-readable immigrant visa (MRIV) to denote temporary evidence of lawful permanent residence. Sometimes, if no foreign passport is available, USCIS will place the I-551 stamp on a Form I-94 and affix a photograph of the bearer to the form. This document is considered a receipt.

Reverify the employee in Section 3 of Form I-9 when the stamp in the passport expires, or one year after the issuance date if the stamp does not include an expiration date. For temporary I-551 receipts, at the end of the receipt validity period, the individual must present the Permanent Resident Card (Form I-551) for Section 2 of Form I-9.

The MRIV demonstrates permanent resident status for one year from the date of admission found in the foreign passport that contains the MRIV.

PROCESSED FOR I-551.
TEMPORARY EVIDENCE OF
LAWFUL ADMISSION FOR
PERMANENT RESIDENCE
VALID UNTIL_____
EMPLOYMENT AUTHORIZED

I-551 Stamp

The temporary Form I-551 MRIV is evidence of permanent resident status for one year from the date of admission.

Temporary I-551 printed notation on a machine-readable immigrant visa (MRIV)

Employment Authorization Document (Form I-766)

USCIS issues the Employment Authorization Document (Form I-766) to individuals granted temporary employment authorization in the United States. The card contains the bearer's photograph, fingerprint, card number, Alien number, birth date, and signature, along with a holographic film and the DHS seal. The expiration date is located at the bottom of the card. Cards may contain one of the following notations above the expiration date: "Not Valid for Reentry to U.S.", "Valid for Reentry to U.S." or "Serves as I-512 Advance Parole."

Employment Authorization Document (Form I-766) with notation "NOT VALID FOR REENTRY TO U.S."

Employment Authorization Document (Form I-766) with notation "VALID FOR REENTRY TO U.S."

Previous back of EAD card

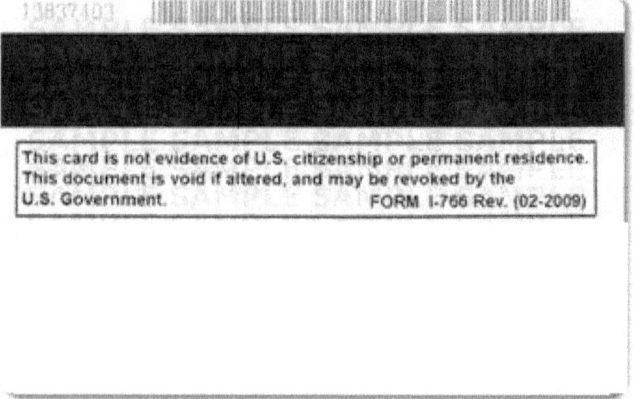

Newly redesigned back of EAD card

Form I-20 Accompanied by Form I-94 or Form I-94A

Form I-94 or Form I-94A for F-1 nonimmigrant students must be accompanied by a Form I-20, *Certificate of Eligibility for Nonimmigrant Students*, endorsed with employment authorization by the designated school official for off-campus employment or curricular practical training. USCIS will issue an Employment Authorization Document (Form I-766) to all students (F-1 and M-1) authorized for a post-completion OPT period.

(See Form I-94 on next page.)

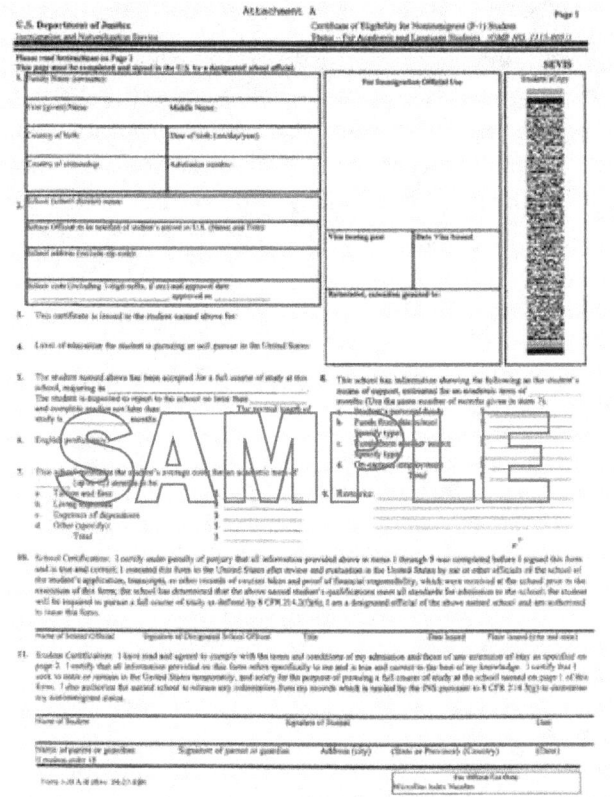

Form I-20 Accompanied
by Form I-94 or Form I-94A

Form DS-2019 Accompanied by Form I-94 or Form I-94A

Nonimmigrant exchange visitors (J-1) must have a Form I-94 or Form I-94A accompanied by an unexpired Form DS-2019, *Certificate of Eligibility for Exchange Visitor (J-1) Status*, issued by the U.S. Department of State, that specifies the sponsor. J-1 exchange visitors working outside the program indicated on the Form DS-2019 also need a letter from their responsible officer.

(See Form I-94 on next page.)

Form DS-2019 Accompanied
by Form I-94 or Form I-94A

Form I-94 or Form I-94A Arrival/Departure Record

CBP and sometimes USCIS issue arrival-departure records to nonimmigrants. This document indicates the bearer's immigration status, the date that the status was granted, and when the status expires. The immigration status notation within the stamp on the card varies according to the status granted, e.g., L-1, F-1, J-1. The Form I-94 has a handwritten date and status, and the Form I-94A has a computer-generated date and status. Both may be presented with documents that Form I-9 specifies are valid only when Form I-94 or Form I-94A also is presented, such as the foreign passport, Form DS-2019, or Form I-20.

Form I-9 provides space for you to record the document number and expiration date for both the passport and Form I-94 or Form I-94A.

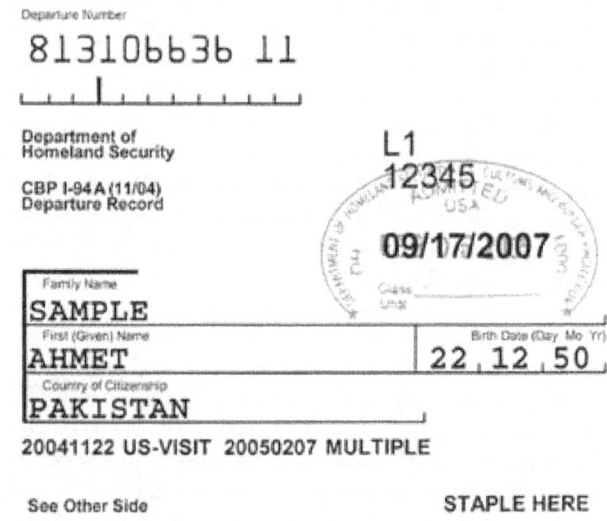

Form I-94 Arrival/Departure Record

Form I-94A Arrival/Departure Record

Passports of the Federated States of Micronesia and the Republic of the Marshall Islands

In 2003, Compacts of Free Association (CFA) between the United States and the Federated States of Micronesia (FSM) and Republic of the Marshall Islands (RMI) were amended to allow citizens of these countries to work in the United States without obtaining an Employment Authorization Document (Form I-766).

For Form I-9 purposes, citizens of these countries may present FSM or RMI passports accompanied by a Form I-94 or Form I-94A indicating nonimmigrant admission under the CFA, which are acceptable documents under List A. The exact notation on Form I-94 or Form I-94A may vary and is subject to change. The notation on Form I-94 or Form I-94A typically states "CFA/FSM" for an FSM citizen and "CFA/MIS" for an RMI citizen.

Passports from the Federated States of Micronesia and the Republic of the Marshall Islands

List B—Documents That Establish Identity Only

State-issued Driver's License

A driver's license can be issued by any state or territory of the United States (including the District of Columbia, Puerto Rico, the U.S. Virgin Islands, Guam, American Samoa, and the Commonwealth of the Northern Mariana Islands) or by a Canadian government authority, and is acceptable if it contains a photograph or other identifying information such as name, date of birth, gender, height, eye color, and address.

Some states may place notations on their drivers' licenses that state the card does not confirm employment authorization. For Form I-9 purposes, these drivers' licenses, along with every other state's, establish the identity of an employee. When presenting any driver's license, the employee must also present a List C document that establishes employment authorization.

State-issued drivers' licenses vary from state to state.

The illustrations below do not necessarily reflect the actual size of the documents.

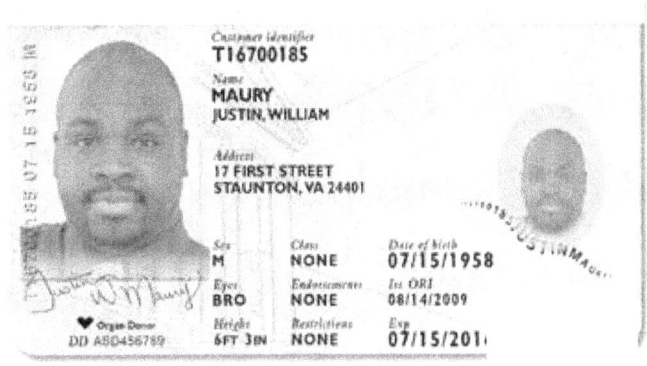

Driver's License from the Commonwealth of Virginia

State-issued ID Card

An ID card can be issued by any state (including the District of Columbia, Puerto Rico, the U.S. Virgin Islands, Guam, American Samoa, and the Commonwealth of the Northern Mariana Islands) or by a local government, and is acceptable if it contains a photograph or other identifying information such as name, date of birth, gender, height, eye color, and address.

Some states may place notations on their ID cards that state the card does not confirm employment authorization. For Form I-9 purposes, these cards, along with every other state's, establish the identity of an employee. When presenting any state-issued ID card, the employee must also present a List C document that establishes employment authorization.

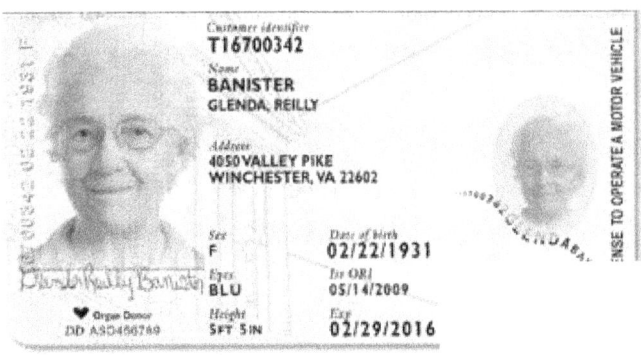

Identification card from the Commonwealth of Virginia

The following illustrations in this Handbook do not necessarily reflect the actual size of the documents.

U.S. Social Security Account Number Card

The U.S. Social Security account number card is issued by the Social Security Administration (older versions were issued by the U.S. Department of Health and Human Services), and can be presented as a List C document unless the card specifies that it does not authorize employment in the United States. Metal or plastic reproductions are not acceptable.

U.S. Social Security Card

Certifications of Birth Issued by the U.S. Department of State

These documents may vary in color and paper used. All will include a raised seal of the office that issued the document, and may contain a watermark and raised printing.

Certification of Birth Abroad Issued by the U.S. Department of State (FS-545)

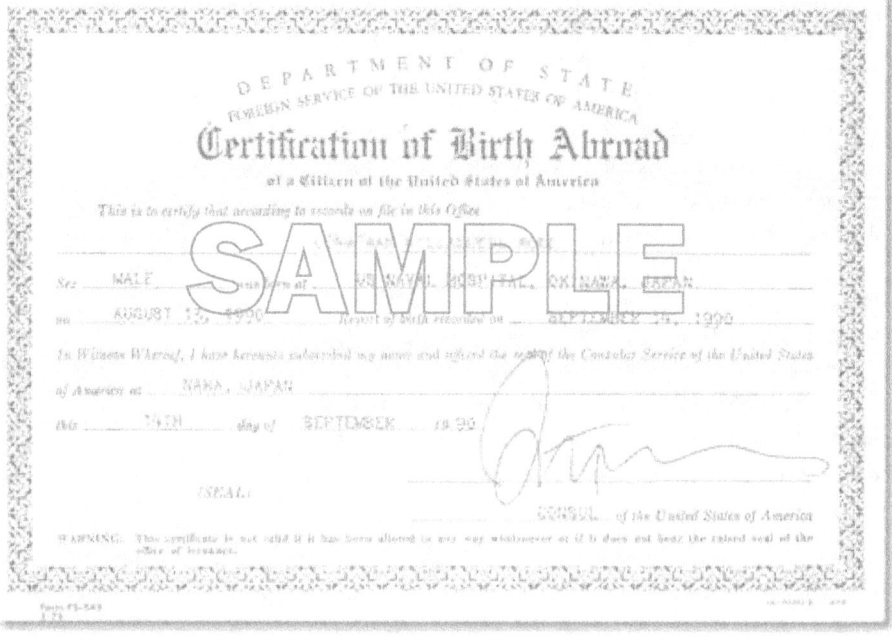

Certification of Report of Birth Issued
by the U.S. Department of State (DS-1350)

Birth Certificate

Only an original or certified copy of a birth certificate issued by a state, county, municipal authority, or outlying possession of the United States that bears an official seal is acceptable. Versions will vary by state and year of birth.

Beginning October 31, 2010, only Puerto Rico birth certificates issued on or after July 1, 2010 are valid. Please check www.uscis.gov for guidance on the validity of Puerto Rico birth certificates for Form I-9 purposes.

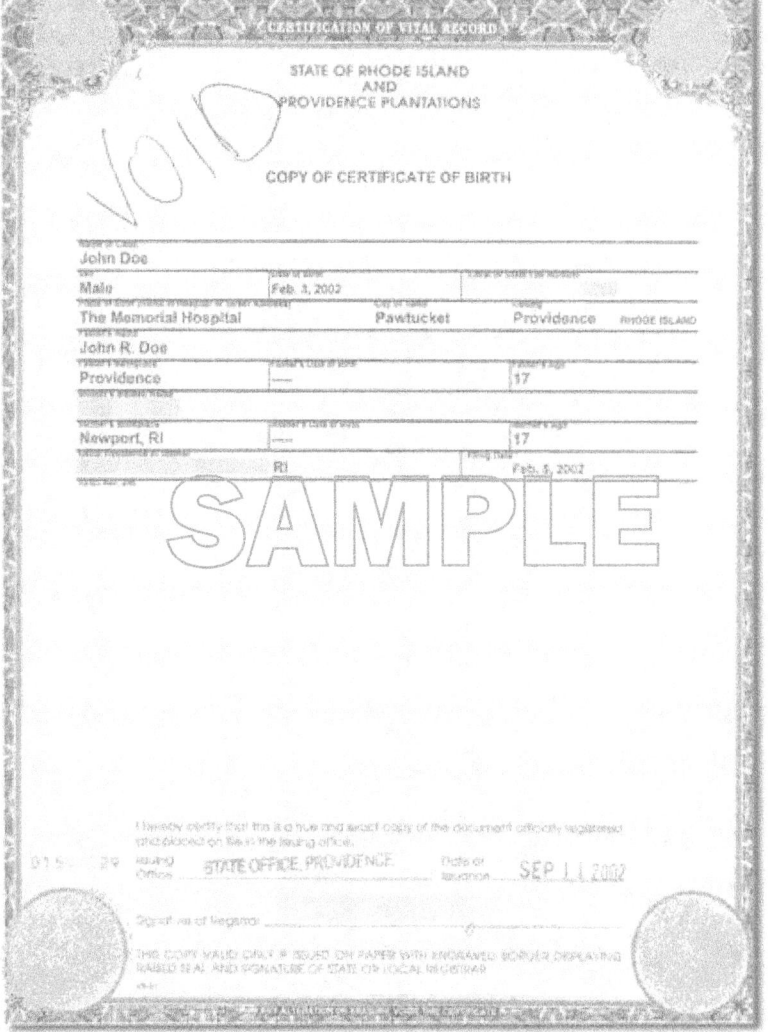

Birth Certificate

U.S. Citizen Identification Card (Form I-197)

Form I-197 was issued by the former Immigration and Naturalization Service (INS) to naturalized U.S. citizens. Although this card is no longer issued, it is valid indefinitely.

U.S. Citizen Identification Card
(Form I-197)

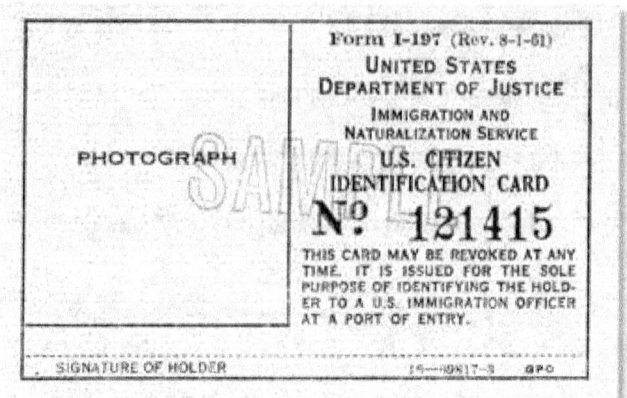

Identification Card for Use of Resident Citizen in the United States (Form I-179)

Form I-179 was issued by INS to U.S. citizens who are residents of the United States. Although this card is no longer issued, it is valid indefinitely.

Identification Card for Use of Resident Citizen in the United States (Form I-179)

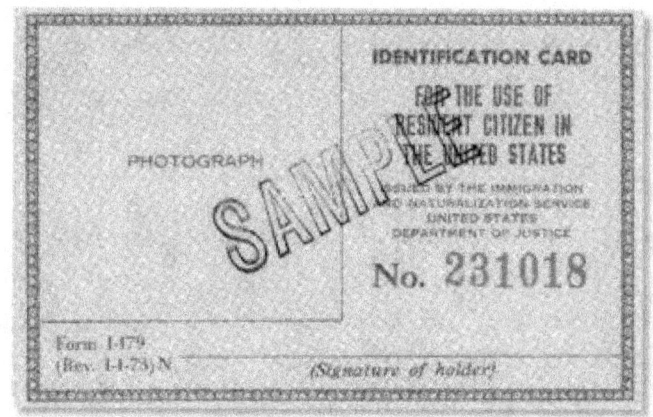